D1321031

WEIRD BUSINESS ™

Edited by
Joe R. Lansdale
and
Richard Klaw

MOJO PRESS

Austin, Texas

PO Box 140005
Austin, TX 78754
mojo@eden.com

Copyright © and TM 1995 Joe R. Lansdale and Richard Klaw

All copyrights are hereby assigned to individual creators.

All rights reseved. No part of this book may be reproduced, in any form or by any means, without the permission in writing from the publisher or the individual copyright holders except for review purposes.

Printed in Canada.

First Printing

1-885418-02-7

The editors and publisher would like to dedicate Weird Business to the memory of Robert Bloch.

———————————————————

The publisher would also like to dedicate this book to Cooter, without whom none of this would have been possible.

Thanks to the following people for information, advice, and just general help and support: Mike Friedrich, Bob Wayne, Lou Stathis, Shirley Klaw, Karen Lansdale, Dalena LeBlanc, and Judy Ostrander.

Special thanks to John Lucas, Newt Manwich, and Ted Naifeh for helping us in our times of need.

Table Of Contents

Introduction

Here in your wet little palms you hold an exciting volume of wonderful comic stories. Not ARCHIE style comic stories, mind you, but stories for adults. These babies aren't the sort of comic tales you read when you were a kid. You know, the guys and gals in spandex pants who whip about seventy-lebbin-million bad guys per issue then have two more issues where they wallow in angst and self-pity over their terrible lot in life. And, of course, every damn issue you pick up is a "collector's" item. I mean, sheesh, doesn't anybody buy comics to read anymore? And who says this crap is collectible? See how much you get for that Superman and Lois Lane get married issue now, buckos.

Listen here. What you got with this baby is a real collector's item, but we don't care. Collector's item hell. We want you to read it. There's just too much good stuff here to stick this book in a plastic bag to sell later.

The stories here... Well, we're talking range, Brothers and Sisters, and since I am co-editor with Rick Klaw and there are so many wonderful creators here, I feel I can drop modesty and say, frankly, this is one of the most unusual and outstanding books ever done in the field of comics.

That's right. Back off and hear it again.

This is one of the most unusual and outstanding books ever done in the field of comics.

Big praise, I realize, but considering the incredible line-up of comic creators, prose writers, artists, it's not a claim made lightly.

Not only does WEIRD BUSINESS contain great adaptations of classic tales by Edgar Allan Poe, Ambrose Bierce, and the late, great, Robert Bloch, it contains mostly original material that will, to put it mildly, blow the doors off your Chevy. And that ain't even countin' the marvelous cover by Dave Dorman. One look at that baby, and, if you have any kind of soul, you'll be all over this book like white on rice.

Warm up the Amen corner and listen to a true believer, cause I'm gonna testify.

If you're tired of the same ole business. If you want something unique. If you think comic book swim suit issues are the dumbest thing since Jesse Helms, then here it is, a hot bundle of short stories, a la graphic novel style.

From pure fantasy to dark horror, to humorous whimsy, to noir, to action/adventure and science fiction, this baby is as hot as the Devil's cigar.

You can put that stack of RICHIE RICH comics back, put that Sidney Sheldon back on the shelf in front of that Jackie Collins book. Cause now listen up: What you need ain't that, Brothers and Sisters, what you need is a little WEIRD BUSINESS, and by golly, by gum, here that baby be, fresh and ripe for the pickin'. The bestest, neatest, most original collection of comic stories ever assembled.

I mean, come on. Would I lie?

All right, enough of the righteous celebration. As I said before, the book speaks for itself. Sometimes, it barks for itself. It might even bite you a little, but in the long run you'll love yourself for hearing the noise, taking the wound.

For Rick and myself this has been a labor of love. Well, mostly. We had to shed some writers and artists along the way. Some were just too flakey to work with. Some couldn't meet deadlines. Some said yes but meant no. Some were prima donas. Some didn't meet the standards this book soon established for itself. Some were just plain ole, pure-dee assholes.

But most, ah, they were wonderful. And so were the fruits of their labors.

Speaking of creators, we want to give space to a very special man here. Robert Bloch. We lost Mr. Bloch last year, and though I had only spoken with him a few times and exchanged some cards and brief letters, it was easy to discern that here was a wonderful human being, as well as one of the most incredible and special talents to ever write in the field of suspense and fantastic literature.

We are honored to have been given permission by Mr. Bloch shortly before his death to include his classic, award-winning story "That Hellbound Train" here in our anthology of comic adapted stories. We believe the adaptors, Neal Barrett, Jr. (writer) and Phil Hester (artist), have outdone themselves in being faithful to Mr. Bloch's creation. We like to think if Mr. Bloch could hold this book in his hands, read his story, that he would be more than satisfied with our rendition of his classic.

In that spirit, we dedicate this book to the inimitable Robert Bloch. A man whose spirit and talent have inspired many of us to make writing our life's work.

So, to your memory, Mr. Bloch, our sincerest respect and gratitude.

Now it is time for me to get out of the way and let you to it.

Enjoy. For the likes of this unique anthology will not come your way again any time soon.

Joe R. Lansdale (his ownself)

Gorilla Gunslinger

Having recently completed his fiftieth short story, *Norman Partridge* is one of the most creative new writers in the country. His first collection of short stories, *Mr. Fox & Other Feral Tales* (Roadkill Press), won the prestigious Bram Stoker award. *Slippin' Into Darkness* (CD Publications 1994), Norman's first novel, will be published in paperback in 1995 from Zebra. Future projects include an anthology of drive-in movie tales, which he will co-edit, a new novel, and hopefully more comic book scripts.

Noted for his extensive research, *John Garcia's* work has appeared in *Owlhoots* (Kitchen Sink), *Medal Of Honor* (Dark Horse), and *Two Fisted Tales* (Dark Horse). Watch for more of John's masterful artwork in *The Wild West Show* from Mojo Press.

GORILLA GUNSLINGER!

ARIZONA TERRITORY, 1874

THE NAME'S KILIMANJARO, THOUGH MOST FOLKS IN THESE PARTS KNOW ME AS MONJO. I'VE BEEN THREE YEARS IN AMERICA. TWO OF THEM WITH MR. P.T. BARNUM. ONE ON MY OWN...UNLESS YOU WANT TO COUNT MY HORSE, THAT IS...

...I COME FROM AN OLD LAND. SOME FOLKS CALL IT THE **DARK CONTINENT.** SAME DIMWITS WHO CALL THIS PLACE THE **NEW FRONTIER...**

... BUT EVEN A CHUCKLEHEADED PRAIRIE DOG CAN SEE THAT THERE AIN'T MUCH NEW ABOUT THIS LAND

STORY: NORMAN PARTRIDGE
LETTERING: DOUG POTTER

...THE LAND HAS ALWAYS BEEN HERE...

...WE'RE THE CURRENT TENANTS, SURE...

...BUT THE RENT'S PAST DUE...

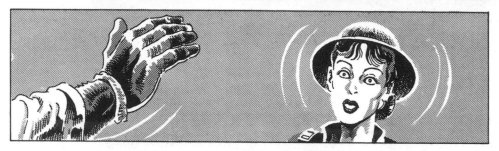

...AND WHILE I'D LIKE TO BELIEVE THAT THERE'S ROOM ENOUGH FOR ALL OF US...

...IN THE LONG RUN, I AIN'T SURE ANY OF IT MATTERS MUCH...

...CAUSE WHEN THE BULLET LEAVES THE CHAMBER...

...WE AIN'T MUCH MORE THAN TOMORROW'S BONES...

...IF WE LAST THAT LONG, THAT IS.

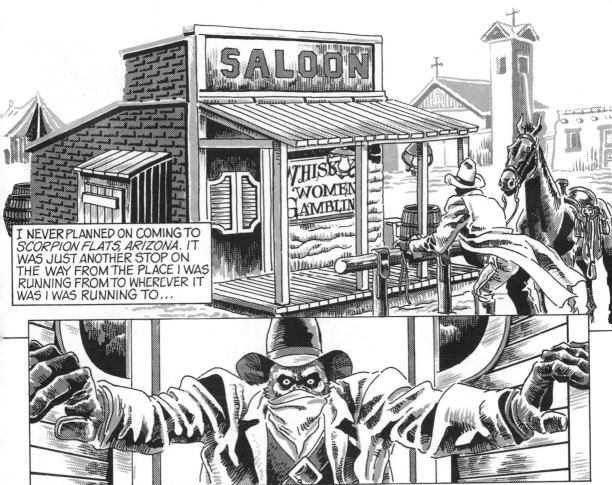

I NEVER PLANNED ON COMING TO *SCORPION FLATS, ARIZONA.* IT WAS JUST ANOTHER STOP ON THE WAY FROM THE PLACE I WAS RUNNING FROM TO WHEREVER IT WAS I WAS RUNNING TO...

WHAT'LL IT BE, STRANGER?

BUCKET OF BEER SHOULD ABOUT DO ME.

UH...WE'RE FRESH OUT OF BEER. THAT'S A FACT. AND THE OTHER FACT IS WE DON'T SERVE NO--

AFRICANS?

NO PROBLEM WITH AFRICANS, FRIEND. **FUGITIVE DESPERADOS**, NOW THAT'S ANOTHER STORY.

ANTED

MONJO

aka PRINCE KILIMA

IRDERER • HORSE-T

$ 10,000 AI

OT ONE DAMN PEN

BUY ME A BEER AND I'LL EXPLAIN EVERYTHING...

IT'S A GOOD STORY--

--ALL ABOUT A VERY UNIQUE TRIBE OF GORILLAS WHO LIVED PEACEFULLY IN AN UNDISCOVERED VALLEY THAT ONE DAY WAS INVADED BY PLUNDERERS--

-- WHO TOOK A YOUNG PRISONER, BUT DIDN'T UNDERSTAND HIS VALUE UNTIL THEY SOLD HIM TO A CIRCUS AND HE SWORE AT THEM IN A LANGUAGE NO HUMAN HAD EVER HEARD--

@$‼₰!

OF COURSE, LATER ON, HE WISHED HE'D KEPT HIS YAP SHUT--

BARNU & PRESENTS
PRINCE KILIMAN
THE ELOQUENT AF

OUT OF THE FRYIN' PAN AND STRAIGHT INTO THE FIRE IS HOW YOU MIGHT PUT IT--

BUT ONE DAY A COUPLE OF BOZOS MADE A BIG MISTAKE --

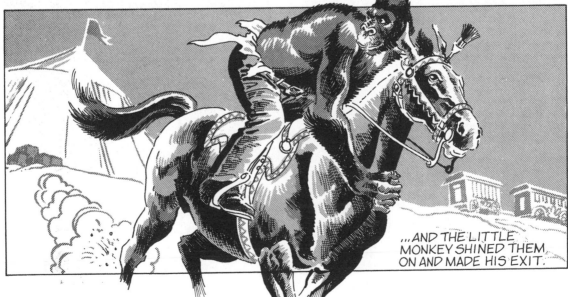

...AND THE LITTLE MONKEY SHINED THEM ON AND MADE HIS EXIT.

LIKE I SAY, IT'S A GOOD STORY, AND I'VE WORKED UP A POWERFUL--

WE DON'T HAVE TIME FOR FAIRY TALES, BANANA-BREATH--

C'MON, KNUCKLE-DRAGGER.

WE'VE GOT A BALLOON OUT-SIDE.

MR. BARNUM'S GONNA BE REAL GLAD TO SEE YOU AGAIN.

WELL, FLEMMO, GOBBO, AND HEMMRO. YOU BOYS LOOK ABOUT AS PERT AS THREE RUTTIN' BUCKS. I GUESS IT WOULD BE KIND OF SILLY TO TELL YOU--

--THAT I'M FEELIN' REAL PEACEABLE TODAY.

HA! HA! HA! THAT WOULD BE SILLY, WOULDN'T IT, BOYS?

BLAM! BLAM! BLAM! BLAM!

CRACKERJACK SHOOTING... FOR A WOMAN.

YOU DO ALL RIGHT YOURSELF. FOR AN APE, I MEAN.

OUCH!

MY NAME'S NEVADA PINE ...AND MY LATE HUSBAND WAS A CAVALRY CAPTAIN. HE TAUGHT ME HOW TO SHOOT. WHAT'S YOUR STORY?

NO STORY AT ALL. GRACIAS AND ADIOS ABOUT SAYS IT.

WAIT!

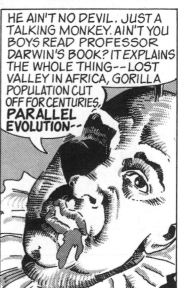

LET'S BE ABOUT THE LORD'S BUSINESS, BROTHERS.

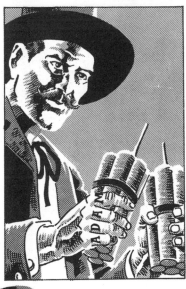

Becoming The Monster

Poppy Z. Brite is the award-winning author of the novels *Lost Souls* and *Drawing Blood* as well as numerous short stories. She has recently completed her new novel, *Exquisite Corpse*, a tale of serial killers. Her first short story collection, *Swamp Foetus,* was published in 1994 by Borderlands Press.

After illustrating the covers to Poppy's first two novels, *Miran Kim* was a natural to draw Poppy's first comic story. Miran's beautiful work has appeared in *Hellraiser* (Marvel), *Star Wars II Trading Cards* (Topps), and *Vertigo Trading Cards* (DC). She is currently doing the covers for *X-Files* (Topps).

BECOMING THE MONSTER

Even now,
your face
still
haunts my dreams.

WRITER : POPPY Z. BRITE
ARTIST : MIRAN KIM

Boys were going missing all over town.

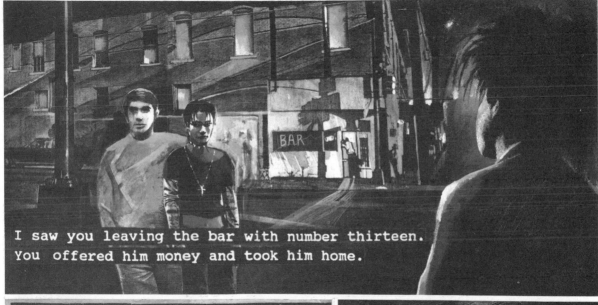

I saw you leaving the bar with number thirteen.
You offered him money and took him home.

I didn't know what you were doing to him in there. Not yet.

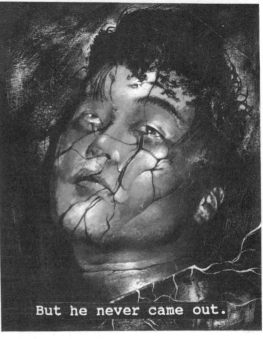

But he never came out.

That was when I knew I had to meet you.

I searched your trash to make sure I was right.

I was.

That night I dreamed of being shot several times in the head.

I remained conscious and felt the bullets lodging in the meat of my brain.

It was very erotic.

As I woke up and masturbated, I thought of men who had killed with guns.

But somehow I didn't think guns would be your kick.

Right again.

I found an envelope with your name on it in the trash.

From that,
I was able to get your phone number,
your work history,
your credit rating...

...and your police record.
Eighteen months' probation
for enticing a minor.

I wanted to be enticed.

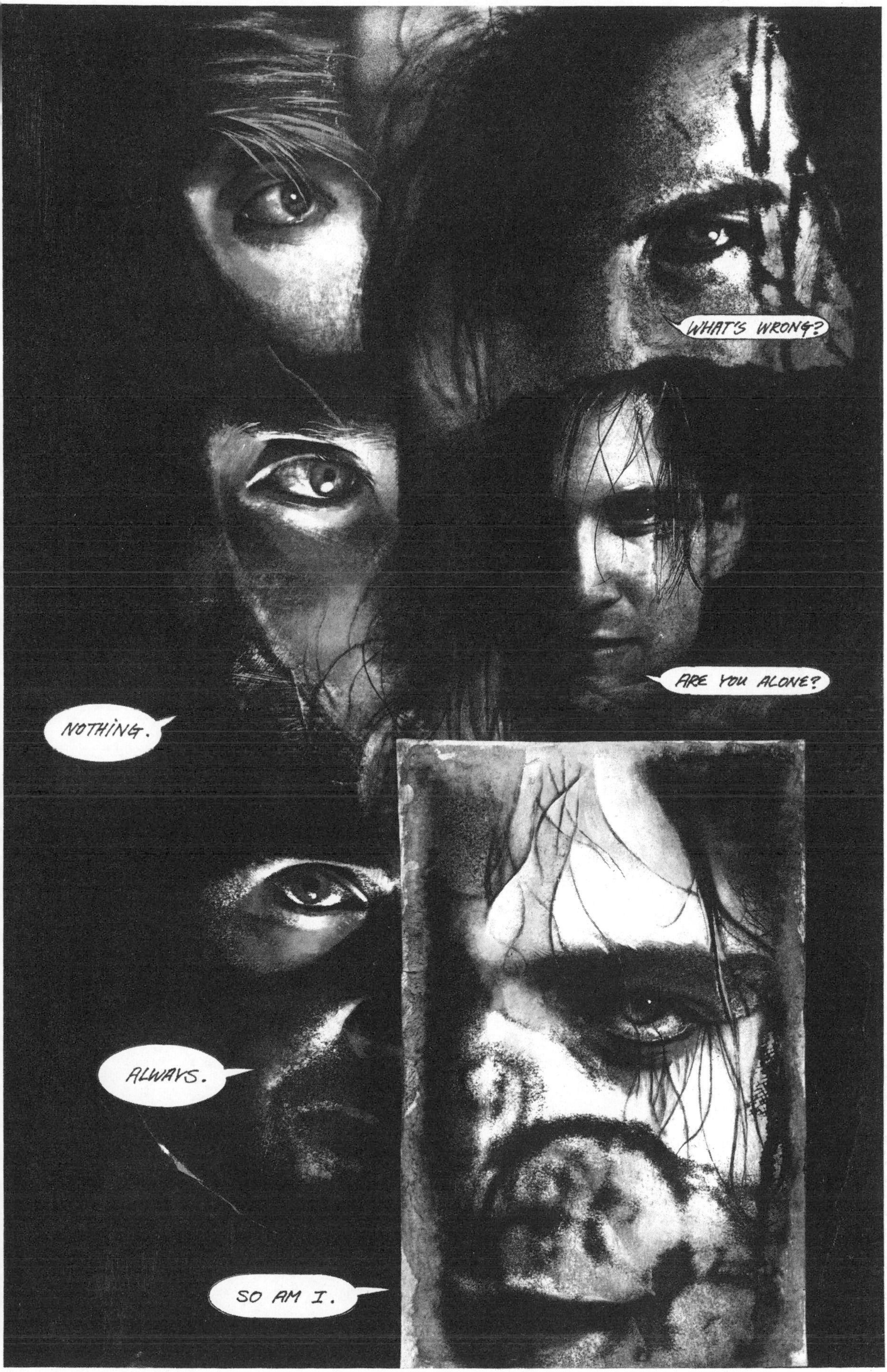
WHAT'S WRONG?
NOTHING.
ARE YOU ALONE?
ALWAYS.
SO AM I.

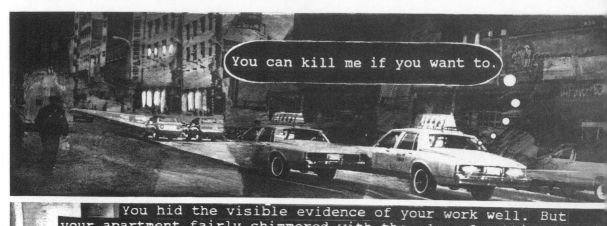

You can kill me if you want to.

You hid the visible evidence of your work well. But your apartment fairly shimmered with the odor of rotting meat. I guessed you hadn't taken out the garbage.

SO WHAT DO YOU DO?

I CRACK SYSTEMS.

WHAT?

I BREAK INTO COMPUTERS. SOMETIMES I DO IT FOR FUN. SOMETIMES PEOPLE PAY ME TO DO IT. I HAVE MY TALENTS.

YOU CRACK SYSTEMS TOO, DON'T YOU?

SO DO I.

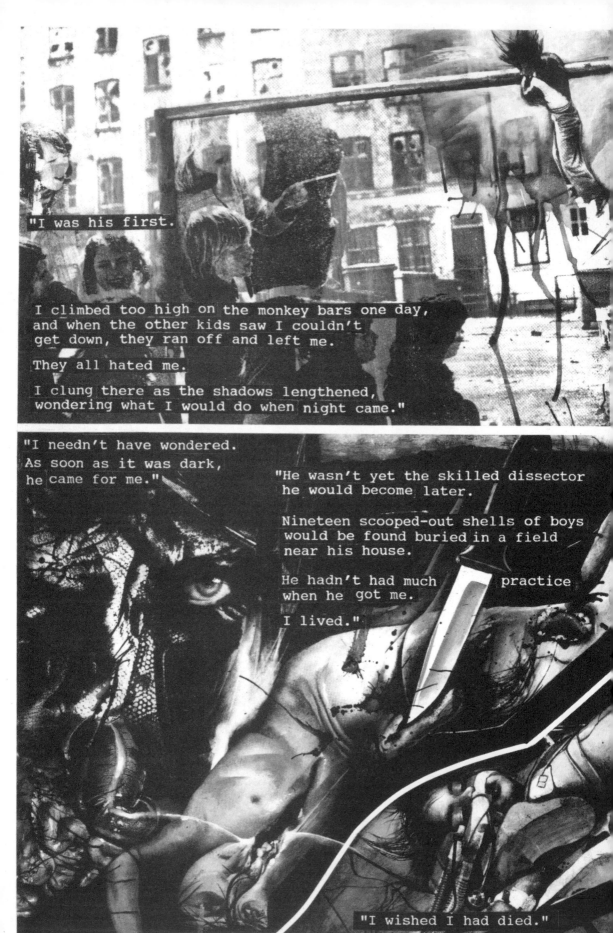

"I was his first.

I climbed too high on the monkey bars one day, and when the other kids saw I couldn't get down, they ran off and left me.

They all hated me.

I clung there as the shadows lengthened, wondering what I would do when night came."

"I needn't have wondered. As soon as it was dark, he came for me."

"He wasn't yet the skilled dissector he would become later.

Nineteen scooped-out shells of boys would be found buried in a field near his house.

He hadn't had much   practice when he got me.

I lived."

"I wished I had died."

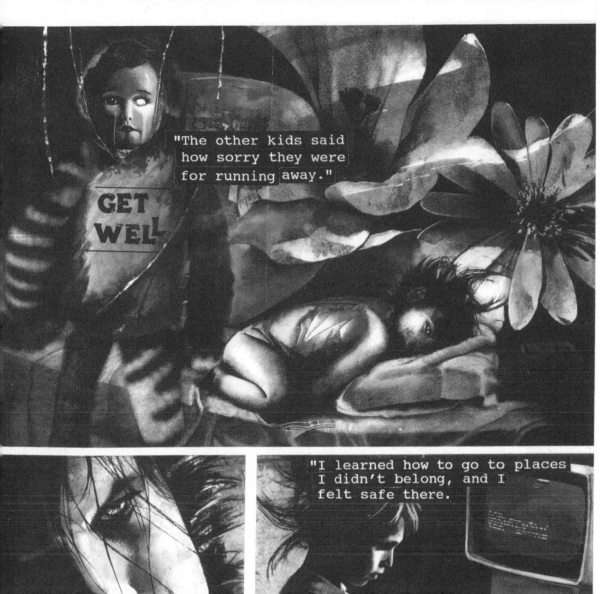

"The other kids said how sorry they were for running away."

GET WELL

"As soon as I could talk, I told them to fuck off."

"I learned how to go to places I didn't belong, and I felt safe there.

Kids couldn't go many places in the real world, and I now knew that most of the places they could go were unsafe."

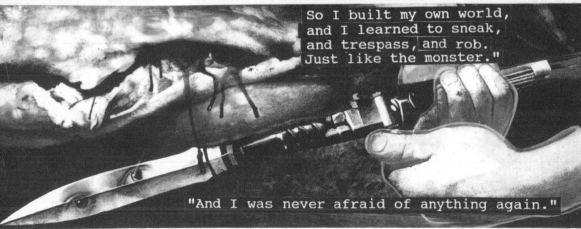

So I built my own world, and I learned to sneak, and trespass, and rob. Just like the monster."

"And I was never afraid of anything again."

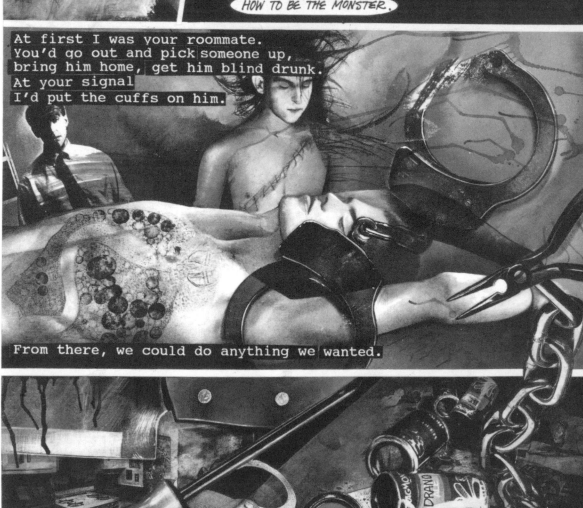

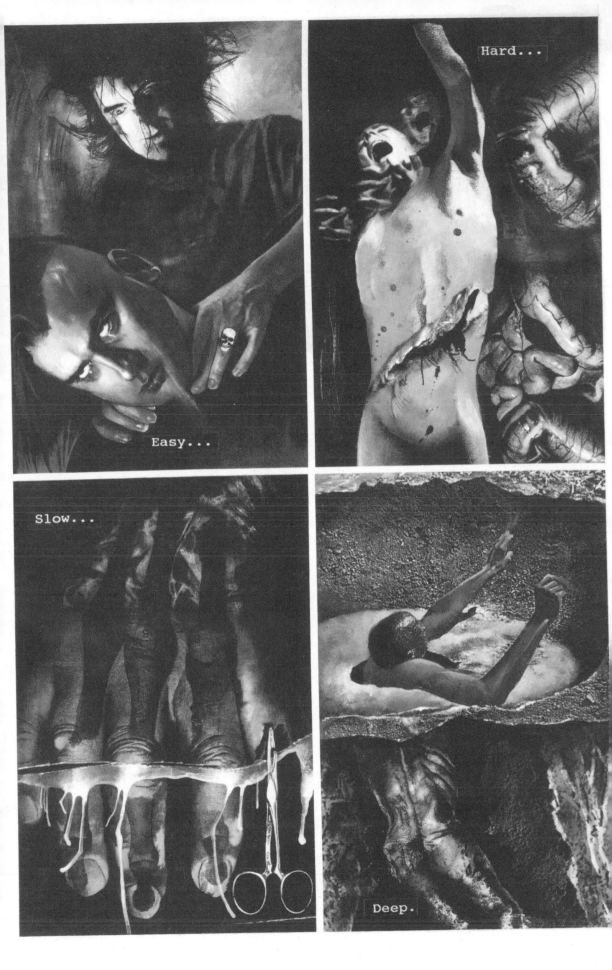

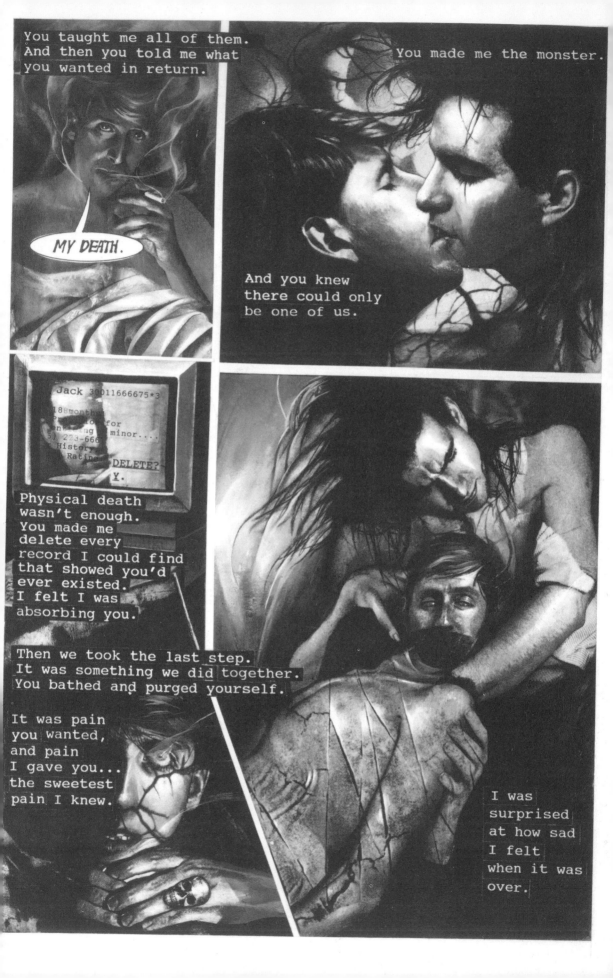

And even now,
your face still haunts
my dreams.

the end.

Till The Cows Come Home

This story is long in coming for Mark Evans. He first showed the original short story to Rick Klaw over six years ago when they worked in a bookstore together. It took some time but finally Rick was good to his word and saw that Mark's vision saw print. This is his first published story.

First coming to prominence as the cover artist for *Book Of The SubGenius*, *Kenneth Huey* has illustrated stories for *Commies From Mars* and *Creature Features* (Mojo Press). He currently lives with his wife in the Seattle area.

BUT I KIN TELL YA, IT SHORE DID TASTE *GOOD*. WE WAS DIGGIN' INTA THICK OL' STEAKS AN' MASH 'TATIES AN' GRAVY...

'CEPT *GRAMPS*, WHO ET NOTHIN' BUT APPLE PIE SINCE HE GOT *DENTURES*.

WE WAS HAVIN' A FINE OL' TIME, WHEN WE COMMENCED TO HEAR THIS BIG *RUCKUS*. ME AN' SISSY RUN UP TO TH' *WINDER* T' SEE WHAT IT WAS, AN' *LORDY*, BUT IT WAS A *MARVEL*.

STREET LOOKED LIKE A WILD WEST *CATTLE DRIVE*, COWS EVVYWHERE. THING WAS, IT SEEMED LIKE THEY WAS CHASIN' FOLKS DOWN. AN' WHEN PEOPLE *FELL*, THEY *DIDN'T* GET BACK UP.

THAT'S NOT *ALL*, NO SIRREE.

THERE WAS THIS LI'L *BEETLE CAR*, SLOWLY DRIVIN' THRU THE HERD – ALL WRAPPED IN *TINFOIL* AN' SPROUTIN' THE DANGEDEST *ANTENNA* I EVER SAW.

2

IT PULLED RIGHT UP T' THE RESTAURANT, AN' OUT JUMPS *HOSEA FERGUSON*— HE CLUMB UP ON TOP AN' STARTED SCREAMIN' AN' DANCIN' LIKE NOTHIN' I EVER SEEN BEFORE.

NOW, DON'T LET THIS GET *BACK* T' MR. FERGUSON, BUT IN THEM DAYS WE ALL FIGGERED HIM FER *CRAZY*. I BEEN DOWN T' TH' JUNKYARD WHERE HE LIVED, AN' I SEEN HIM WRAP HISSELF UP IN WIRE AN' WAIT FER *LIGHTNIN'* T' STRIKE— ONCET HE SIT IN A IGLOO O' CAR BATTERIES TILL HIS SMELL ALONE LIKE T' KNOCK YA DOWN.

LORD KNOWS WHAT HE'D GOT IN HIS HEAD *THIS* TIME.

HE WAS WAVIN' HIS ARMS AN' HOWLIN' LIKE A SNAKEBIT DOG. SUDDENLY, I SEES ALL THEM COWS IS LOOKIN' WHERE HE'S POINTIN' WHICH IS RIGHT *MY WAY!* AN' I *SHIVERED* WHEN I UNNERSTOOD WHAT HE WAS *YELLIN'.*

BEEEF! BBBEEEEFFFFF!!

AFORE I KNOWED IT, TH' WINDER'S *FULL* O' COWS LOOKIN' IN, AN' I SWEAR, TH' SIGHT 'BOUT MADE ME PEE MY PANTS!

ALL-YOU-CAN-EAT STEAK SPECIAL .99

3

AN' HOSEA'S POINTIN' A *REMOTE CONTROL* AT 'EM — THAT'S WHEN I NOTICED THEY ALL HAD *FOIL* AN' *WIRE* WRAPPED 'ROUND THEIR HORNS, AN' *RADIOS* AN' STUFF.

KEE-FASSH!

HE *STARES* AT 'EM REAL HARD, AN' NEXT THING I KNEW, THEM BIGGEST BULLS WAS *CRASHIN'* THRU TH' FRONT O' TH' REST'RANT AN' COMIN' STRAIGHT AT US!

SONNY, YOU NEVER *SEEN* SUCH A MESS AS THEM BEEVES MADE O' THET PLACE! SMASHIN' UP FURNITURE AN' BUSTIN' THRU WALLS—

BUT WHAT WAS *WUST* WAS WHEN THEY SAW THE *MEAT LOCKER* IN BACK. THET'S WHEN THEY TURNED AROUND AN' MADE OL' BILLY RAY GALORE, THE OWNER, INTO *HAMBURGER*.

NO, SONNY...

YEW DON'T REALLY WANNA *KNOW* WHAT "HAMBURGER" WAS.

4

AFTER A WHILE, THE COWS GOT STARTED ROUNDIN' US HUMANS UP INTO TH' STREET.

TH' WAY THEY ACTED WHEN HOSEA WENT TO BELLOWIN' OUT "LEATHERRR!!" IT WASN'T TOO LONG AFORE EVVYONE WAS PULLIN' OFF THEIR *BOOTS* AN' *BELTS* AN' TOSSIN' 'EM INTO A BIG PILE.

THEY WOULDN'T LEAVE REV. & MRS. BAKER *ALONE* TILL THEY GOT OUT O' THIS FUNNY *UNDERWEAR* THEY HAD ON.

THEM COWS STARTED SNIFFIN' FOLKS, *BUTTIN'* TH' HOLDOUTS, TILL THET PILE WAS COVERED WITH *WALLETS* AN' *PURSES.*

THEN HOSEA GOES SLOPPIN' *GAS* ON THET PILE O' LEATHER, KINDA *CROONIN'* AN' *CAPERIN'* ALL TH' WHILE.

AN' THEN HE SET IT ON *FIRE.* THE COWS WAS LOOKIN' SO *SOLEMN* THAT ALL TH' FOLKS GOT REAL *QUIET*—'CEPT FER HOSEA FERGUSON, WHO'S STILL MAKIN' A NOISE FIT TO WAKE TH' *DAID.*

AFTER TH' FIRE BURNED OUT, I NEVER *SEEN* A NIGHT SO DARK AN' *FEARFUL.* ALL NIGHT LONG THEY WAS GLASS BREAKIN' AN' COWS BAWLIN' AN' SOMETIMES A *SCREAM*— AN' US WONDERIN' WHAT THOSE COWS WAS GONNA DO *NEXT.*

5

Steel Valentine

Award-winning author, black belt, and father, *Joe R. Lansdale* is one of the most unique writing talents in the country. Joe has written 12 novels, over 200 short stories, five comic book mini-series, a juvenile book, three episodes of *Batman: The Animated Series,* and a host of other things. In comics he has written the award-winning *Jonah Hex: Two Gun Mojo* (DC/Vertigo), *Lone Ranger & Tonto* (Topps), and *Jonah Hex: Riders Of The Worm and Such* (DC/Vertigo). His short work has been adapted for *By Bizarre Hands* (Dark Horse), *System Shock* (Tuscany Press), and *The Wild West Show* (Mojo Press). Upcoming comic projects include *Blood & Shadows* (DC/Vertigo) and a new *Lone Ranger & Tonto* series from Topps.

Richard Klaw has previously adapted Joe R. Lansdale and Dan Lowry's "Pilots" for *System Shock* (Tuscany Press). He lives in Austin, Texas, with his wife and her two cats.

A real hidden talent, *Marc Erickson* is an artist of fantastic quality and wonderful temperament. His previous work includes an issue of *By Bizarre Hands* (Dark Horse), and stories in *Negative Burn* (Caliber Press). Watch for his new *Houdini* story in *Negative Burn.*

The STEEL Valentine

BY JOE R. LANSDALE
SCRIPT BY RICHARD KLAW
ART BY MARC ERICKSON
LETTERS BY BRAD THOMTE

EVEN BEFORE MORLEY TOLD HIM, DENNIS KNEW THINGS WERE ABOUT TO GET UGLY.

A MAN DID NOT CLUB YOU UNCONSCIOUS, BRING YOU TO HIS ESTATE AND TIE YOU TO A CHAIR IN AN EMPTY STORAGE SHED OUT BACK OF THE PLACE IF HE MERELY INTENDED TO GIVE YOU A VALENTINE.

MORLEY HAD FOUND OUT ABOUT HIM AND JULIE.

HE TRIED TO SILENTLY WORK THE ROPES LOOSE.

IF HE COULD GET FREE, MAYBE...

THERE WOULD STILL BE THE STRAND HOLDING HIS ANKLES TO THE CHAIR, BUT MAYBE IT WOULDN'T TAKE TOO LONG TO UNDO THAT. AND EVEN IF IT DID, IT WAS AT LEAST SOME KIND OF PLAN.

IF HE GOT THE CHANCE TO GO ONE ON ONE WITH MORLEY, HE MIGHT TAKE HIM. HE WAS TWENTY-FIVE YEARS YOUNGER AND IN GOOD SHAPE HIMSELF. NOT AS GOOD AS WHEN HE WAS PLAYING PRO BASKETBALL, BUT GOOD SHAPE NONETHELESS.

HE HAD HEIGHT, REACH, AND HE STILL HAD WIND. HE KEPT THE LATTER WITH PLENTY OF JOGGING AND TOSS-ING THE SPECIAL-MADE, SIXTY-FIVE POUND MEDICINE BALL AROUND WITH RAUL.

STILL, MORLEY WAS STRONG. PLENTY STRONG. DENNIS COULD TESTIFY TO THAT. THE PULSAT-ING KNOT ON THE SIDE OF HIS HEAD WAS THERE TO REMIND HIM.

BEEN, WHAT A WEEK SINCE YOU'VE SEEN YOUR PRECIOUS SWEETHEART?

AM I RIGHT?

DENNIS DID NOT ANSWER, BUT MORLEY WAS RIGHT.

HE HAD GONE BACK TO THE STATES FOR A WHILE TO SETTLE SOME MATTERS, GET PART OF HIS INHERITANCE OUT OF LEGAL BONDAGE SO HE COULD COME BACK, GET JULIE, AND TAKE HER TO THE STATES FOR GOOD. HE WAS TIRED OF THE MEXICAN HEAT AND TIRED OF MORLEY OWNING THE WOMAN HE LOVED.

IT WAS JULIE WHO HAD ARRANGED FOR HIM TO MEET MORLEY IN THE FIRST PLACE, AND PROBABLY EVEN THEN THE OLD BASTARD HAD SUSPECTED.

AND FROM THE FIRST MOMENT DENNIS MET HIM, HE KNEW HE HAD TO GET JULIE AWAY FROM HIM.

IT WASN'T THAT MORLEY WAS OPENLY ABUSIVE— IN FACT, HE WAS THE PERFECT HOST ALL THE WHILE DENNIS WAS THERE— BUT THERE WAS AN OBVIOUS UNDER-CURRENT OF CONNUBIAL DOMINANCE THAT REVEALED ITSELF LIKE A SHARK FIN EVERYTIME HE LOOKED AT JULIE.

STILL, IN A STRANGE WAY, DENNIS FOUND MORLEY INTERESTING, IF NOT LIKABLE. HE WAS A BRIGHT AND INTRIGUING TALKER, AND A WIZARD AT CHESS. BUT WHEN THEY PLAYED AND MORLEY TOOK A PIECE, HE SMIRKED IN SUCH A WAY AS TO MAKE YOU FEEL HE ACTUALLY VANQUISHED AN OPPONENT.

THE SECOND AND LAST TIME DENNIS VISITED THE HOUSE WAS THE NIGHT BEFORE HE LEFT FOR THE STATES.

I CAN'T TAKE HIM MUCH LONGER.

I KNOW. SEE YOU IN ABOUT A WEEK. AND IT'LL ALL BE OVER.

"THIS WAS INVENTED BY SOME BUSINESS ASSOCIATE OF MINE. IT CAME OUT OF SOME CHEMICAL WARFARE RESEARCH I'M CONDUCTING. I'M IN, SHALL WE SAY... ESPIONAGE? I WORK FOR THE HIGHEST BIDDER. I HAVE PLANTS HERE FOR ARMS AND CHEMICAL WARFARE."

"IF IT'S PROFITABLE AND UGLY, I'M INVOLVED. I'M A REAL STINKER SOMETIMES, I CERTAINLY AM."

"WE CAME UP WITH THIS TO TRAIN ATTACK DOGS. WE FOUND WE COULD SPRAY A PADDED UP MAN WITH THIS AND THE DOGS WOULD GO BONKERS. RIP THE PADS RIGHT OFF OF HIM. SOMETIMES THE ONLY WAY TO STOP THE BEGGERS WAS TO SHOOT THEM."

"IT WAS A FAILURE ACTUALLY. IT ACTIVATED THE DOGS, BUT IT DROVE THEM OUT OF THEIR MINDS AND THEY COULDN'T BE CONTROLLED AT ALL. AND AFTER A SHORT TIME THE ODOR FADED, AND THE SPRAY BECAME QUITE THE REVERSE. IT MADE IT SO THE DOGS COULDN'T SMELL THE SPRAY AT ALL. IT MADE WHOEVER WAS WEARING IT ODORLESS."

"STILL I FOUND A PERSONAL USE FOR IT. A VERY PERSONAL USE."

"I LET CHUM GO A FEW DAYS WITHOUT FOOD AND WATER WHILE I WORKED ON JULIE."

"AND SHE WASN'T TOUGH AT ALL. NOT EVEN ONE LITTLE BIT. SPILLED HER GUTS. NOW THAT ISN'T ENTIRELY CORRECT. SHE DIDN'T SPILL HER GUTS UNTIL LATER, WHEN CHUM GOT A HOLD OF HER."

"ANYWAY, SHE TOLD ME WHAT I WANTED TO KNOW ABOUT YOU TWO, THEN I SPRAYED THAT DELICATE THIRTY-SIX, TWENTY-FOUR, THIRTY-SIX, FIGURE OF HERS WITH THIS."

"WITH CHUM SO HUNGRY, AND ME HAVING BURNED HIS FEET AND DONE SOME MEAN THINGS TO HIM, HE WAS NOT IN THE BEST OF HUMOR WHEN I GAVE HIM JULIE."

"IT WAS DISGUSTING. REALLY. I HAD TO COME BACK WHEN IT WAS OVER AND SHOOT CHUM WITH A TRANQUILIZER DART, GET HIM TIED AND MUZZLED FOR YOUR ARRIVAL."

"I SUPPOSE IT ISN'T POLITE TO LECTURE A CAPTIVE AUDIENCE, BUT I THOUGHT YOU MIGHT LIKE TO KNOW A FEW THINGS ABOUT DOGS. NO NEED TO TAKE NOTES. YOU WON'T BE AROUND FOR A QUIZ LATER."

HE'S PROBABLY NOT HUNGRY NOW, BUT THIS WILL STILL DRIVE HIM CRAZY.

HERE'S SOME THINGS TO TUCK IN THE BACK OF YOUR MIND WHILE YOU AND CHUM ARE ALONE. DOGS ARE VERY STRONG. VERY. THEY LOOK SMALL COMPARED TO A MAN, BUT THEY EXERT A LOT OF PRESSURE WITH THEIR BITE. I'VE SEEN DOGS LIKE CHUM HERE BITE THROUGH THE THICKER END OF A BASEBALL BAT. AND THEY'RE QUICK. YOU'D STAND A BETTER CHANCE AGAINST A BLACK BELT IN KARATE THAN AN ATTACK DOG.

MORLEY, YOU CAN'T DO THIS.

I CAN'T? NO, I BELIEVE I CAN. I GIVE MYSELF PERMISSION.

BUT HEY, DENNIS, I'M GOING TO GIVE YOU A CHANCE. THIS IS THE GOOD PART NOW, SO LISTEN UP. YOU'RE A SPORTING MAN. BASKETBALL, RACQUETBALL, CHESS, ANOTHER MAN'S WOMAN. SO YOU'LL LIKE THIS. THIS WILL APPEAL TO YOUR SENSE OF COMPETITON.

HAHAHAHA!

DENNIS COULDN'T BELIEVE HOW STRONG THE DOG WAS. SIXTY POUNDS OF PURE MUSCLE AND ENERGY.

SIXTY POUNDS OF MUSCLE.

THE MEDICINE BALL AT THE GYM WEIGHED MORE.

SORRY.

HE WONDERED ABOUT THE OTHER
DOBERMANS. WONDERED IF MORLEY
KILLED THEM TOO, OR IF HE WAS
KEEPING THEM AROUND. THE DOBER-
MANS WERE USUALLY LOOSE ON
THE YARD AT NIGHT.

HADN'T MORLEY SAID THAT LATER
ON THE SPRAY KILLED A MAN'S
SCENT? THAT WAS SOMETHING;
IT COULD BE THE EDGE HE NEEDED.

BUT IT DIDN'T REALLY MATTER.
NOTHING MATTERED ANYMORE.
SIX DOGS. SIX WAR ELEPHANTS.
HE WAS GOING AFTER MORLEY.

OUTSIDE THE STUDY DOOR, IN THE HALL, HE COULD HEAR JULIE'S DOGS PADDING NERVOUSLY. THEY WANTED OUT. HE HATED THOSE BASTARDS, AND JUST MAYBE HE'D GET RID OF THEM. SHOOT THEM AND INSTALL A BURGLAR ALARM. ALARMS DIDN'T HAVE TO EAT OR BE LET OUT TO SHIT, AND THEY WOULDN'T TURN ON YOU.

HE HEARD A SOUND, LIKE SOMETHING BEING DRAGGED ACROSS THE GRAVEL DRIVE. HE SAT MOTIONLESS A MOMENT, NOT BATTING AN EYE. IT COULDN'T BE LOVER BOY, HE THOUGHT. NO WAY.

I'VE GOT MONEY.

FUCK YOUR MONEY. I'M NOT SELLING ANYTHING HERE. GET UP AND GET OVER HERE.

THERE, NOW.

Stranger

Often compared to Charles Addams and Edward Gorey, *Brian Biggs* first unleashed his bizarre storytelling skills on an unsuspecting world with the love story *Frederick & Eloise* (Fantagraphics). Since then Brian's work has appeared in a variety of magazines. He is currently in negotiations for his new graphic novel, *Dear Julia.*

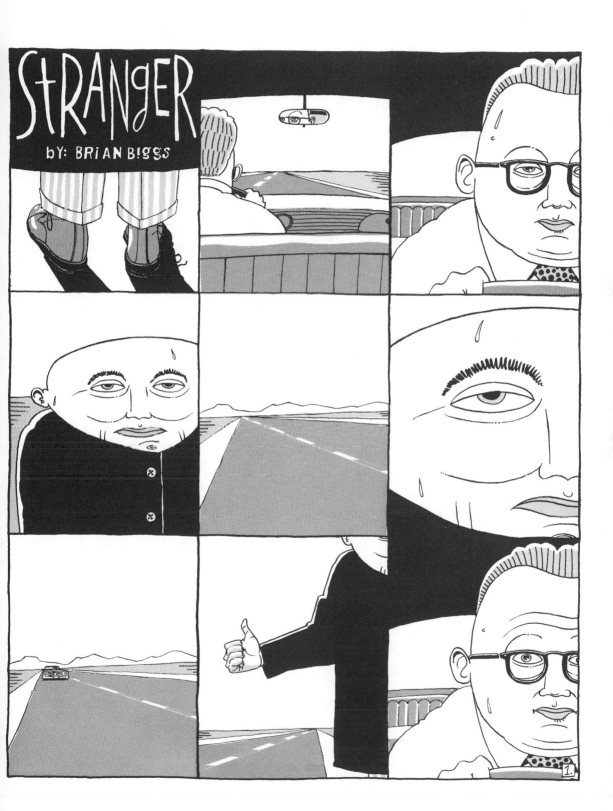

That Hell-Bound Train

A beloved master of horror and mysteries, *Robert Bloch*'s writing career spanned more than forty years. During that period he created such classics as *Psycho*, "Yours Truly, Jack The Ripper," and the story adapted here. "That Hell-Bound Train" is the penultimate "deal with the devil" story and the winner of the 1959 Hugo award for best short story.

A writer who has written and excelled in almost every genre imaginable, *Neal Barrett, Jr.* was the first and best choice to adapt this classic tale.

Phillip Hester has worked on books for several companies including Tundra, Dark Horse, Marvel, Caliber, DC and others. His hauntingly original art can be seen currently in *Swamp Thing* (DC/Vertigo), *Argus* (DC), *Boneshaker* (Caliber), and *Negative Burn* (Caliber).

A frequent contributor to many of Malibu's books, Iowa based *Andre Walls* is self-publishing his book *Courage, Inc.* under the Forefront banner.

Ande Parks has worked on several projects with *Phil Hester* including *Nightbreed* (Marvel), *Rust* (Malibu), *Fringe* (Caliber), and *Freaks' Amour* (Dark Horse). Currently he inks *Anima*, *Steel*, and *Superboy*, all for DC.

THAT HELL-BOUND TRAIN

by **ROBERT BLOCH**

ADAPTED BY.... NEAL BARRETT, Jr.
ART BY......... PHILLIP HESTER
ANDE PARKS and
ANDREW WALLS
LETTERS BY..... GARY PETERSON

— *FOR ROBERT* —

WHEN MARTIN WAS LITTLE, HIS DADDY WAS A RAILROAD MAN. HE WALKED THE TRACKS FOR THE CB&Q, AND EVERY NIGHT HE GOT DRUNK AND SANG THIS OLD SONG ABOUT *THAT HELL-BOUND TRAIN*...

ONE NIGHT, MARTIN'S DADDY GOT *REAL* DRUNK, AND GOT HIMSELF SQUEEZED BETWEEN A PENNSY TANK CAR AND AN AT&SF GONDOLA. NOT LONG AFTER THAT, MOM RAN OFF WITH A SALESMAN FROM KEOKUK, AND MARTIN ENDED UP IN THE LOCAL ORPHAN'S HOME.

MARTIN DIDN'T CARE FOR THE ORPHAN LIFE. HE RAN OFF AS SOON AS HE COULD, AND TOOK TO THE OPEN ROAD. EVERY NIGHT, AFTER THE OTHER BINDLESTIFFS WERE ASLEEP, HE'D SOFTLY HUM HIS DADDY'S OLD SONG.

IT TOOK MARTIN FOUR OR FIVE YEARS, A HUNDRED AND NINE ODD JOBS, AND SIX MONTHS ON AN ALABAMA CHAIN GANG, TO FIGURE OUT THERE WASN'T ANY FUTURE IN DRIFTING AROUND THE COUNTRY ON HIS OWN...

1

HE TRIED TO GET ON WITH THE RAILROAD LIKE HIS DADDY, BUT TIMES WERE PRETTY BAD. "IF I CAN'T WORK FOR THEM, I'LL KEEP ON *RIDING* 'EM," MARTIN DECIDED. AND HE DID.

RAILROADING WAS PURELY IN HIS BLOOD. HE'D RATHER HOP A FREIGHT HEADING NORTH IN SUB-ZERO WEATHER, THAN LIFT HIS THUMB TO HITCH A RIDE WITH A CADILLAC HEADED FOR FLORIDA.

AND EVERY NIGHT HE'D THINK ABOUT **THAT HELL-BOUND TRAIN.** THE TRAIN THE DRUNKS AND SINNERS RODE-- THE GAMBLERS, THE SKIRT CHASERS, THE BIG-TIME SPENDERS---

IT WOULD BE REAL FINE TO TAKE A TRIP IN SUCH GOOD COMPANY, BUT MARTIN DIDN'T LIKE TO THINK OF WHAT HAPPENED WHEN THAT TRAIN FINALLY PULLED INTO THE DEPOT WAY DOWN YONDER...

HE DIDN'T FIGURE ON SPENDING ETERNITY STOKING THE BOILERS IN HELL, WITHOUT EVEN A COMPANY UNION TO PROTECT HIM. STILL, IT WOULD BE A LOVELY RIDE, IF THERE WAS SUCH A THING AS A HELL-BOUND TRAIN. WHICH, OF COURSE, THERE WASN'T...

AT LEAST, MARTIN DIDN'T THINK THERE WAS, UNTIL THAT COLD NOVEMBER NIGHT IN THE FOX RIVER VALLEY, WHEN HE HEARD THAT WHISTLE SCREAMING OUT OF THE BLACK THROAT OF THE NIGHT, SCREAMING LIKE A LOST AND LONELY SOUL...

AND THEN THE TRAIN WAS RIGHT ON TOP OF HIM; A BIG BLACK PASSENGER TRAIN WITHOUT A SINGLE LIGHT IN THE LONG STRING OF CARS.

MARTIN WAS SURE THIS TRAIN DIDN'T BELONG TO THE NORTH-WESTERN ROAD. CERTAIN IT DIDN'T WHEN THE CONDUCTOR CLAMBERED DOWN FROM THE FORWARD CAR...

...HELD THE DARK LANTERN UP TO HIS MOUTH AND BLEW IT INTO A FIERY RED GLOW.

MARTIN FELT THIS WAS A MIGHTY PECULIAR THING TO DO, BUT HE TRIED TO REMEMBER HIS MANNERS WHEN THE CONDUCTOR APPROACHED HIM AND NEARLY TIPPED HIS CAP.

WELL, GOOD EVENING, MARTIN.

GOOD EVENING, MR. CONDUCTOR.

UH, HOW DID YOU KNOW MY NAME?

HOW DID YOU KNOW I WAS THE CONDUCTOR?

YOU *ARE* AREN'T YOU?

TO YOU, YES. THOUGH OTHER PEOPLE MAY RECOGNIZE ME IN DIFFERENT ROLES.

YOU OUGHT TO SEE WHAT I LOOK LIKE TO THE FOLKS OUT IN HOLLYWOOD.

YEAH? AND WHAT BRINGS YOU HERE?

WHY, I CAME BECAUSE I FELT YOU NEEDED ME, MARTIN. I CAME TO OFFER YOU A *RIDE*.

I'M NOT SURE I'D CARE TO RIDE YOUR TRAIN, SIR. CONSIDERING WHERE I'M LIKELY TO END UP.

AH, YES, THE OLD ARGUMENT. I SUPPOSE YOU'D PREFER SOME SORT OF *BARGAIN*, IS THAT IT?

5

SO THAT'S ALL THERE IS TO IT, *huh*?

ABSOLUTELY. BUT REMEMBER, YOU ONLY GET TO STOP THE WATCH *ONCE*. I CAUTION YOU IN ALL FAIRNESS--MAKE SURE YOU'RE SATISFIED WITH THE MOMENT YOU CHOOSE TO PROLONG.

SINCE YOU'VE BEEN SO *FAIR* WITH ME, I OUGHT TO TELL YOU THERE'S ONE THING YOU'VE FORGOTTEN. IT DOESN'T MATTER *WHAT* MOMENT I CHOOSE, BECAUSE ONCE I STOP TIME FOR MYSELF, I STAY WHERE I AM FOREVER. I'LL NEVER GET ANY OLDER AND I'LL NEVER DIE. AND IF I NEVER DIE, I'LL NEVER HAVE TO RIDE ON YOUR TRAIN.

OH, DEAR. AND *I'M* SUPPOSED TO BE THE TRICKY ONE!

SSSSHAAAAAAAH!

MARTIN WAS PLEASED WITH HIMSELF. HE KNEW HE'D MADE A FOOLPROOF DEAL WITH MR. CONDUCTOR. A HELL OF A DEAL, SO TO SPEAK. HE'D HAD NO REAL DESTINATION IN MIND BEFORE, BUT HE HAD ONE NOW. HE WAS GOING TO FIND A MOMENT OF HAPPINESS...

TWO DAYS LATER MARTIN WAS IN THE GREAT CITY OF CHICAGO. DRIFTING OVER TO WEST MADISON STREET, HE TOOK STEPS AT ONCE TO ELEVATE HIS LIFE. HE BECAME A CITY BUM, A PANHANDLER, A MOOCHER.

A WHOLE DIME? GOD BLESS YOU, SIR.

IT DIDN'T TAKE LONG BEFORE HAPPINESS WAS A TWO-BIT FLOP AND A FIFTH OF MUSCATEL. MARTIN EVEN THOUGHT OF UNWINDING HIS WATCH AT THE PEAK OF INTOXICATION. DID IT GET ANY BETTER THAN THIS?

MARTIN DECIDED IT DID. HE THOUGHT ABOUT ALL THE HONEST JOHNS HE'D BRACED FOR A HANDOUT THAT DAY. SURE, THEY WERE SQUARES, BUT THEY WERE PROSPEROUS, TOO. THEY WORE GOOD CLOTHES, AND DROVE NICE CARS...

THEY ATE DINNER IN FINE HOTELS, SLEPT ON INNER-SPRING MATTRESSES, AND DRANK BLENDED WHISKEY. THERE WAS MORE HAPPINESS OUT THERE, AND MARTIN WENT TO SLEEP DETERMINED TO GET SOME FOR HIMSELF...

DINER

BEFORE THE MONTH WAS OUT, MARTIN WAS WORKING FOR A CONTRACTOR ON THE SOUTH SIDE. HE HATED THE GRIND, BUT THE PAY WAS GOOD. HE SLEPT IN A COMFORTABLE BED AND WENT DOWN TO THE CORNER TAVERN EVERY SATURDAY NIGHT.

WORK. FOR FOOD

IT WASN'T LONG BEFORE A RAISE CAME THROUGH. A RAISE MEANT A SECONDHAND CAR, AND A CAR MEANT -- GIRLS!

THE FIRST TIME A COUPLE OF GIRLS CAME THROUGH, MARTIN WANTED TO UNWIND HIS WATCH **IMMEDIATELY**. THEN HE GOT TO THINKING WHAT A GUY AT WORK SAID...

"... YOU CAN RUN AROUND WITH PIGS WHEN YOU'RE YOUNG, BUT AFTER A WHILE, YOU WANT TO GET A **NICE** GIRL OF YOUR OWN." MARTIN THOUGHT THE GUY WAS PROBABLY NUTS, BUT MAYBE HE'D GIVE IT A TRY.

12
9
3
6

Happy New Year!

IN SIX MONTHS, MARTIN WAS PROMOTED AGAIN. NOW HE WAS WORKING **INSIDE**, IN THE OFFICE, AND TAKING BOOKKEEPING AT NIGHT. THAT'S WHEN HE MET LILLIAN GILLIS.

LILLIAN **WAS** LOTS OF FUN, BUT SHE WAS A NICE GIRL TOO, AND TOLD MARTIN THEY'D HAVE TO WAIT UNTIL THEY WERE MARRIED TO DO YOU-KNOW-WHAT. MARTIN KNEW SHE WAS WORTH IT-- BUT HE THOUGHT ABOUT HIS BIMBOS A LOT...

LILLIAN **WAS** WORTH WAITING FOR, AND THEN SOME.

MARTIN THOUGHT ABOUT HIS WATCH. MAYBE NOW WAS THE TIME... JUST A FEW TWISTS AND-- **ZAP!** PERMANENT SATISFACTION WITH HIS FORMERLY BLUSHING BRIDE.

MARRIAGE HAD A FEW SURPRISES IN STORE. LILLIAN WANTED A NICE NEW HOUSE. MARTIN WANTED A GOOD TV. THERE WAS AN EXTRA MOUTH TO FEED, AND THAT MEANT NIGHT COURSES AGAIN.

IT TOOK A LITTLE TIME, BUT MARTIN MADE IT. HE CLOSED A BIG DEAL, THEN ANOTHER AND ANOTHER AFTER THAT. BY THE TIME YOUNG MARTIN JUNIOR WAS IN HIGH SCHOOL, MARTIN WAS RETIRED.

MARTIN HAD A HUNCH THAT EVENING THAT IT WAS NOW OR NEVER. HIS LIFE WAS FULL AND RICH, AND HE WASN'T EXACTLY A KID ANYMORE.

...BUT RIGHT ABOUT THEN HE MET SHERRY WESTCOTT. SHERRY TAUGHT HIM A TOUPEE WOULD COVER THE BALD SPOT AND A CUMBERBUND COULD COVER THE POT. IN FACT, SHE TAUGHT HIM QUITE A LOT. AND HE SO ENJOYED LEARNING THAT HE ACTUALLY TOOK OUT HIS WATCH AND PREPARED TO UNWIND IT.

UNFORTUNATELY, HE CHOSE THE VERY INSTANT THAT THE PRIVATE DETECTIVES BROKE DOWN THE DOOR OF THE HOTEL ROOM. AND THEN THERE WAS A LONG STRETCH OF TIME WHEN MARTIN COULDN'T SAY HE WAS REALLY *ENJOYING* ANY GIVEN MOMENT.

AFTER THE FINAL DIVORCE SETTLEMENT WITH LIL, HE WAS BROKE AGAIN... AND SHERRY WESTCOTT DIDN'T SEEM TO THINK HE LOOKED ALL THAT GREAT AFTER ALL.

MARTIN SQUARED HIS SHOULDERS AND WENT BACK TO WORK. EVENTUALLY, HE MADE HIS PILE AGAIN — BUT IT TOOK LONGER THIS TIME, AND THERE WASN'T ANY CHANCE TO HAVE FUN ALONG THE WAY.

HE WASN'T INTERESTED IN THE FANCY DAMES OR THE EXPENSIVE BOOZE ANYMORE. BUT THERE WERE OTHER PLEASURES FOR THE RICH. TRAVEL, FOR INSTANCE — AND NOT THE KIND OF TRAVEL WHERE YOU RIDE THE RAILS FROM ONE HICK BURG TO ANOTHER, EITHER...

ON ONE MAGIC NIGHT, HE FELT HE HAD FOUND HIS PERFECT MOMENT AFTER ALL. STILL, IF HE STOPPED TIME NOW, HE REALIZED HE'D BE ALL ALONE. LIL AND THE KID WERE GONE. SHERRY WAS GONE. AND HE'D NEVER HAD TIME TO MAKE FRIENDS.

THAT MUST BE THE ANSWER, HE DECIDED. IT WASN'T JUST MONEY OR POWER OR SEX OR SEEING BEAUTIFUL THINGS. THE REAL SATISFACTION LAY IN FRIENDSHIP.

ON THE BOAT TRIP HOME, HE TRIED TO STRIKE UP CONVERSATIONS AT THE BAR. BUT ALL THESE PEOPLE WERE YOUNGER, AND MARTIN HAD NOTHING IN COMMON WITH THEM.

MAYBE THAT'S WHY HE HAD HIS "LITTLE ACCIDENT" THE DAY BEFORE THEY DOCKED IN SAN FRANCISCO. THAT'S WHAT THE SHIP'S DOCTOR LIKED TO CALL IT, BUT MARTIN KNEW BETTER THAN THAT...

ALL THE EXPENSIVE TREATMENT AND ALL THE EXPENSIVE DOCTOR SMILES DIDN'T FOOL MARTIN AT ALL. HE WAS AN OLD MAN WITH A BAD HEART, AND THEY THOUGHT HE WAS GOING TO DIE.

BUT MARTIN KNEW HE COULD FOOL THEM. HE STILL HAD HIS WATCH -- HE COULD CHEAT DEATH WITH A SINGLE GESTURE, AND HE INTENDED TO DO IT AS A FREE MAN, OUT THERE UNDER A FREE SKY.

THAT WAS THE REAL SECRET OF HAPPINESS. HE UNDERSTOOD IT NOW. NOT EVEN FRIENDSHIP MEANT AS MUCH AS FREEDOM. THAT WAS THE BEST THING OF ALL -- TO BE FREE OF FRIENDS OR FAMILY OR THE FURIES OF THE FLESH.

COME TO THINK OF .T, HE WAS JUST ABOUT BACK WHERE HE'D STARTED SO MANY YEARS AGO. BUT THE MOMENT WAS GOOD, GOOD ENOUGH TO PROLONG FOREVER. ONCE A BUM, ALWAYS A BUM, MARTIN SMILED TO HIMSELF.

HE TOOK ONE STEP AND THEN ANOTHER AND THE SMILE TWISTED INTO SOMETHING AWFUL, SOMETHING HURTFUL AND BAD, LIKE A KNIFE TWISTING SHARPLY IN HIS CHEST...

NO ONE HAD TO TELL HIM WHAT HAPPENED. IT WAS ANOTHER STROKE, AND A BAD ONE. HE COULD **NOT** PLAY THE FOOL ANY LONGER. NOW WAS THE TIME TO USE HIS POWER AND SAVE HIS LIFE.

A FEW TWISTS AND HE'D CHEAT DEATH -- HE'D NEVER HAVE TO RIDE THAT HELL-BOUND TRAIN. HE COULD GO ON FOREVER...

FOREVER...? DID HE WANT TO GO ON FOREVER; A SICK OLD MAN LYING HELPLESSLY IN THE GRASS? NO, HE COULDN'T; HE WOULDN'T! AND SUDDENLY HE WANTED TO CRY, BECAUSE HE KNEW THAT SOMEWHERE ALONG THE LINE HE'D OUTSMARTED HIMSELF...

HE KNEW BECAUSE HE COULD ALREADY HEAR THAT DISTANT AND SORROWFUL SOUND; THAT FAR-OFF ROARING IN THE NIGHT...

...THE DREADFUL ROAR OF THAT HELL-BOUND TRAIN.

"HELLO, MARTIN," THE CONDUCTOR SAID. "ALL ABOARD!"

I KNOW. BUT YOU'LL HAVE TO CARRY ME. I CAN'T WALK.

I'M-- NOT REALLY TALKING ANYMORE, AM I?

YES YOU ARE. I CAN HEAR YOU JUST *FINE*.

AND YOU CAN *WALK* TOO!

-- MINUTE...

AND THERE THEY ALL WERE: THE DRUNKS AND THE SINNERS; THE GRIFTERS AND THE BIG-TIME SPENDERS; THE SKIRT-CHASERS AND THE GAMBLERS. THEY KNEW WHERE THEY WERE GOING AND THEY DIDN'T GIVE A DAMN.

THEY WERE TOO BUSY LAUGHING AND JOKING AND HAVING FUN -- JUST THE WAY MARTIN'S DADDY USED TO SING ABOUT THEM IN HIS SONG...

MIGHTY NICE TRAVELING COMPANIONS. WHY, I'VE NEVER SEEN SUCH A PLEASANT BUNCH OF PEOPLE!

I'M AFRAID THINGS WON'T BE QUITE AS DELIGHTFUL WHEN WE PULL INTO THAT DEPOT WAY DOWN YONDER.

NOW IF I COULD HAVE THAT WATCH--

A BARGAIN'S A BARGAIN, RIGHT? I AGREED TO RIDE YOUR TRAIN IF I COULD STOP TIME WHEN I FOUND MY PERFECT MOMENT OF HAPPINESS.

I THINK I'M ABOUT AS HAPPY RIGHT HERE AS I'VE EVER BEEN...

CLIK

NO!!

WOOOOOOK!

19

Coccyx

A former Harvey Award nominee, *John Bergin* is an illustrator, designer, and musician. He designed, wrote, and painted the 300 page graphic novel *From Inside* (Kitchen Sink); co-edited, designed, and contributed to the comic and illustrated fiction anthology *Bone Saw* (Tundra); wrote and drew *Ashes* (Caliber); and designed *The Crow (Deluxe Edition)* with a 70 minute CD "soundtrack" by Bergin's musical project *Trust Obey*.

Coccyx

[TH]ERE IS A HORRIBLE PLAGUE [IN] OUR CITY. IT KILLED ME.

IT KILLS INSTANTLY - ALL YOUR MUSCLES RETRACT LIKE STEEL BANDS, YOUR SKIN REVOLTS AND TRIES TO LEAVE YOUR BODY. AND YOUR BLOOD HARDENS, CAUSING YOUR VEINS TO SHOOT FROM YOUR BODY THEN FREEZE LIKE MILLIONS OF RAZOR SHARP ANTENNAS.

I WAS WALKING IN AN ALLEY WHEN THE PLAGUE STRUCK. I STAYED WHERE I FELL UNTIL THE COLLECTORS CAME TO GET ME.

THE COLLECTORS CLEAR PLAGUE VICTIMS FROM THE CITY STREETS.

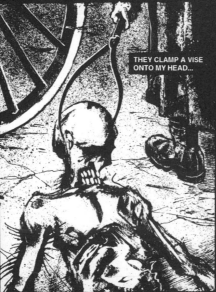

THEY CLAMP A VISE ONTO MY HEAD...

AND UNCEREMONIOUSLY DUMP ME INTO THEIR CART.

EVERYONE MOVES OUT OF THE WAY AS THEY ROLL THROUGH THE CITY.

THE CITY WAS QUITE MODERN ONCE, BUT NOW EVERYTHING IS COVERED WITH MAKESHIFT WOODEN EXTENSIONS, OLD ROPES, GAS LAMPS, NETS, AND RUSTY WIRES.

OCCASIONALLY AN OLD PIECE OF TECHNOLOGY IS DISCOVERED. A FEW PEOPLE HAVE ACCESS TO ELECTRICITY OR AN OLD HOVERCRAFT.

ONCE UPON A TIME THIS CITY WAS A GREAT CITY. I WOULD FIND THAT HARD TO BELIEVE JUDGING FROM THE SEWER IT IS NOW...BUT TWO BUILDINGS FROM THE OLD AGE STILL STAND.

THEY ARE USED FOR RELIGIOUS CEREMONIES.

I HAVE A GOOD VIEW FROM WHERE THEY THREW ME ONTO THE CART.

BENT.

DRESSED IN RAGS.

AS WE SLOWLY WIND DOWN THE STREETS I LOOK AT THE CITIZENS.

THEY ARE ALL SICK.

OPEN SORES.

IT IS ONLY A MATTER OF TIME BEFORE THE PLAGUE KILLS EVERYONE.

BY NIGHTFALL WE REACH
OUR DESTINATION...
THE WASTELAND.

MASSIVE AREA OF SCORCHED EARTH PILED
[H] WITH DEBRIS AND WRECKAGE. ONCE IT
[S] A PARK...NOW IT IS A DUMPING GROUND
[R] PLAGUE VICTIMS.

THE PLACE IS LITTERED WITH BODIES IN
VARIOUS STATES OF DECOMPOSITION.
A FLESHPILE.

THE COLLECTORS EMPTY THEIR
CART AND SPREAD US OUT WITH
PITCHFORKS.

THE NIGHT IS COLD AND WE ARE
STILL WARM. STEAM CONDENSES
FROM OUR BODIES.

WHEN THEY ARE
DONE THEY SLOWLY
TRUNDLE AWAY.

LEAVING US ALONE...
IT IS QUIET. THE MOON IS FULL.

THE WASTELAND IS A MYSTERIOUS
PLACE. THERE ARE MANY STORIES OF
STRANGE ENERGIES THAT HAUNT IT.
GHOSTS, RADIOACTIVE FALLOUT,
RAMPANT ELECTRICAL CURRENTS, AND
MAGNETIC FORCES.

I HEAR A NOISE...

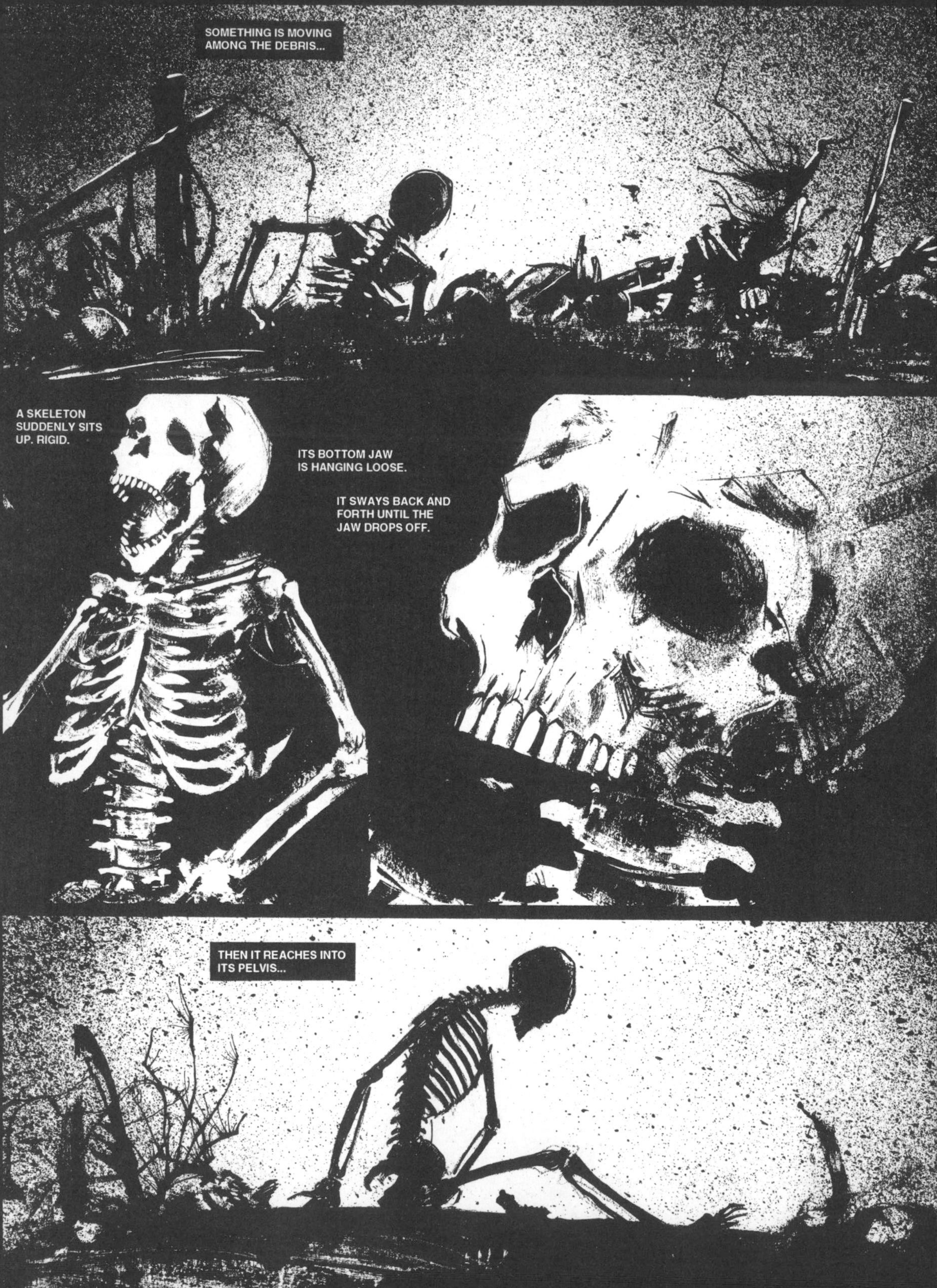
SOMETHING IS MOVING
AMONG THE DEBRIS...
A SKELETON
SUDDENLY SITS
UP. RIGID.
ITS BOTTOM JAW
IS HANGING LOOSE.
IT SWAYS BACK AND
FORTH UNTIL THE
JAW DROPS OFF.
THEN IT REACHES INTO
ITS PELVIS...

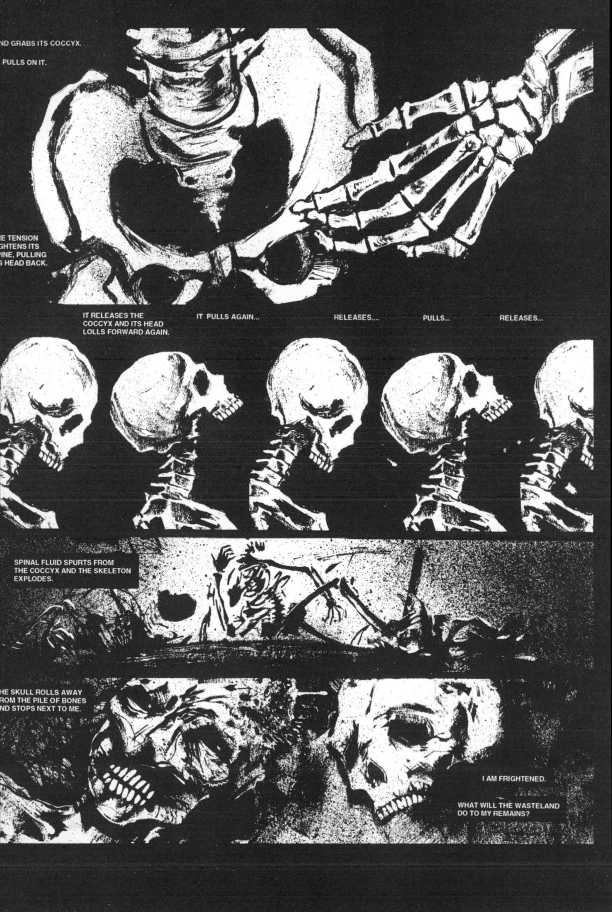

If I Close My Eyes Forever

Novelist, poet, artist, and musician, *Charles de Lint* is one of the most influential fantasy writers of his generation. His works include *Spiritwalk*, *Moonheart*, *Into The Green*, *Dreams Underfoot*, and others. Charles lives in Ottawa, Ontario, Canada, with his wife MaryAnn Harris.

Pia Guerra's pencils have appeared in *Freeflight* (Thinkblots) and *Big Book Of Urban Legends* (DC/Paradox). She is writing and drawing an upcoming issue of *Aeon Focus* (Aeon).

One of the saner residents of Waco, Texas, *William Traxtle* is another one of those unheralded talents. William was one of the founders of Absolute Comics where he inked *Shottloose* and *Punk*, which he co-created. Upcoming works include stories in the *Punk Origin Special* (CFD).

WAS WORKING LATE IN MY
FICE, THE FIRST TIME I MET HER.

...TRYING TO MAKE MYSELF SO
TIRED THAT BY THE TIME I DID
GET HOME, I'D JUST FALL INTO
BED AND SLEEP.

NO, LET'S BE HONEST. I WAS
PUSHING PAPERS AROUND,
KILLING TIME.

ELISE
BORN...
DIED JULY 23
1994
R.I.P.

IF I CLOSE MY EYES FOREVER

Story: Charles de Lint   Pencils: Pia Guerra   Letters: Doug Potter

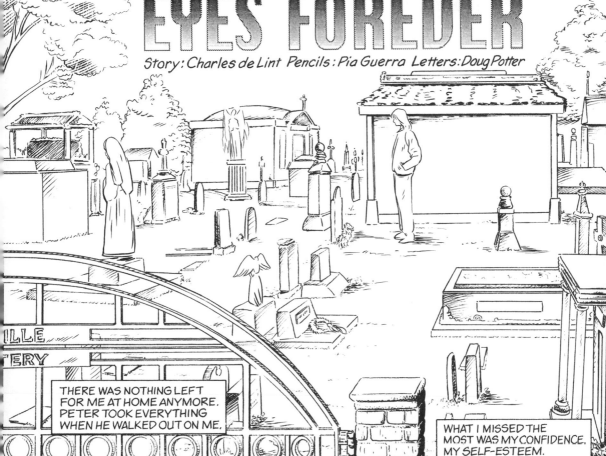

THERE WAS NOTHING LEFT
FOR ME AT HOME ANYMORE.
PETER TOOK EVERYTHING
WHEN HE WALKED OUT ON ME.

WHAT I MISSED THE
MOST WAS MY CONFIDENCE,
MY SELF-ESTEEM.

OH, NO. YOU'VE MISUNDERSTOOD ME. IT'S TRUE WE HAD A RELATIONSHIP, AND IT'S TRUE SHE LEFT ME, BUT I'M NOT LOOKING TO GET HER BACK. I JUST WANT MY HEART BACK. IT'S A PENDANT. SHE TOOK IT WITH HER WHEN SHE LEFT.

THIS IS STILL A JOB FOR A PRIVATE DETECTIVE--OR MAYBE EVEN THE POLICE, IF YOU CAN PROVE OWNERSHIP OF THE STOLEN PROPERTY.

IT'S NOT THAT SIMPLE.

IT NEVER IS, IS IT?

SO TELL ME ABOUT IT.

THIS IS GETTING KINKIER BY THE MINUTE. "SO YOU'RE INTO GAY, OR I GUESS, BISEXUAL GUYS, TOO?"

"NOT AT ALL."

"THE HEART WAS A GIFT TO ME FROM FAERIE."

"HEY, I DON'T HAVE A PROBLEM WITH IT. LIVE AND LET LIVE, I SAY.

"WHEN I SAY FAERIE, I MEAN THE OTHERWORLD. I DID A FAVOR ONCE FOR A PRINCE OF THE REALM AND HE GAVE ME THE PENDANT IN GRATITUDE. IT ALLOWS ONE THE GIFT OF SECOND SIGHT. OF PIERCING THE BARRIERS BETWEEN WHAT WE BELIEVE WE SEE AND WHAT IS ACTUALLY THERE."

SCRATCH THE KINKY, I THINK. THIS WOMAN BELONGS IN A PADDED CELL AT THE ZEB. EXCEPT SHE'S SO EARNEST. I CAN'T HELP BUT LEAN FORWARD AS SHE TALKS, KNOWING IT'S ALL HOGWASH, BUT **WANTING** IT TO BE REAL. I MEAN, HOW MANY OF US DIDN'T GO THROUGH A RAIN-BOW AND UNICORN PHASE WHEN WE WERE ELEVEN OR TWELVE?

NEON SIST

SEE, THE WAY SHE TELLS IT, ONC YOU GET THEIR ATTENTION, ONC THEY KNOW YOU CAN SEE THEM, YOU'VE GOT TO HAVE PROTECTIC OR YOUR ASS IS GRASS. SOUND LIKE LIFE ON THE STREET TO M BUSINESS AS USUAL, EXCEPT SHE'S DESCRIBING CREATURE WITH KNIVES FOR FINGERS AND WORSE.

SO I LET HER RAMBLE ON ABOUT GIFTS FROM THE FAERIE FOLK AND HOW THEY DON'T WORK FOR EVERY-BODY, BUT THEN WHAT DOES? HOW HER PARTICULAR PENDANT NOT ONLY GIVES ITS BEARER THIS SECOND SIGHT, BUT ALSO PROTECTS HER FROM SOME OF THE, SHALL WE SAY, LESS FRIENDLY DENIZENS OF THE OTHERWORLD. THE FRIENDLIES PRETTY MUCH IGNORE YOU, BUT THE OTHERS...

FEEL LIKE I'M TRAPPED IN A VIDEO EDITION OF *THE WEEKEND SUN*, DIRECTED BY ROGER CORMAN--SOMEWHERE BETWEEN "NUN GIVES BIRTH TO PIG TWINS" AND THE ELVIS SPOTTER PAGE--SO WHEN I FIND MYSELF AGREEING TO HELP HER TRACK DOWN HER FRIEND AND THE PENDANT, I STARTLE MYSELF.

I MEAN, THIS REALLY ISN'T MY LINE OF WORK. I'M STRICTLY AN OVER-THE-PHONE GIRL. I DO RESEARCH, GO ELECTRONIC-TRIPPING THROUGH THE ONLINE SERVICES. SOMETIMES I HAVE TO LEAVE THE OFFICE TO WORK THE STACKS AT THE *NEWFORD LIBRARY* OR SOMETHING SIMILAR.

I WOULDN'T KNOW WHERE TO BEGIN TO FIND A MISSING PERSON EXCEPT FROM WHAT I'VE SEEN IN THE MOVIES.

MY NAMELESS CLIENT ISN'T STUMPED. SHE TELLS ME TO HIT THE GIRL BARS ON *GRACIE STREET* AND GIVES ME A PHOTO OF HER FRIEND. SHE TELLS ME SHE'LL BE IN TOUCH WITH ME TOMORROW NIGHT.

LEAVES ME SITTING THERE IN MY OFFICE WONDERING, IF SHE KNOWS HOW TO DO IT SO WELL, WHY SHE'S BOTHERING TO HIRE ME? LEAVES ME WONDERING JUST HOW MUCH PETER'S LEAVING ME HAS SCREWED ME UP THAT I'D AGREE TO DO SOMETHING LIKE THIS.

DON'T KNOW MY CLIENT'S NAME. I DON'T KNOW THE NAME OF THE WOMAN I'M LOOKING FOR. MY HEAD'S SPINNING WITH FAIRY TALES, BUT AT LEAST SHE LEFT HER SMOKES. I GIVE THEM UP EVERY COUPLE OF MONTHS. RIGHT NOW I'M OFF THEM. WAS.

LIVE AND LET LIVE, I THINK, MY EARLIER WORDS TO MY CLIENT COMING BACK TO HAUNT ME. BUT I'VE NEVER BEEN HIT ON SO MANY TIMES IN SUCH A SHORT PERIOD OF TIME AS I HAVE IN THE PAST COUPLE OF HOURS. AND NOT ONCE BY A GUY.

IT REALLY ISN'T A PROBLEM FOR ME. MY BEST FRIEND IN HIGH SCHOOL, SARAH JONES, CAME OUT TO ME IN OUR SENIOR YEAR AND WE'RE STILL GOOD FRIENDS. BUT IT'S HAPPENING SO OFTEN RIGHT NOW THAT I FIND MYSELF WONDERING WHAT IT WOULD BE LIKE TO GO OUT WITH ANOTHER WOMAN.

SO I STUFF THE PACK IN MY POCKET AND HIT THE STREET. IT'S GOING ON ELEVEN, WHICH MEANS THE ACTION'S JUST STARTING ON *GRACIE STREET*.

I TAKE A LOOK AT THESE CIGARETTES MY CLIENT LEFT BEHIND AND WONDER WHAT'S IN THEM, BECAUSE FIRST, SHE HAS ME OUT HERE PLAYING DETECTIVE FOR HER AND NOW I'M ACTUALLY CONSIDERING...

I RECOGNIZE HER, EVEN WITH A BLONDE WIG. SHE LOOKS ENOUGH LIKE ME FROM A DISTANCE THAT I'D BE AMUSED, IF I DIDN'T FEEL A LITTLE SICK. THE LOVIN' SPOONFUL'S "DO YOU BELIEVE IN MAGIC?" IS BLASTING FROM THE SOUND SYSTEM. SHE'S PLAYING THE LITTLE GIRL, LIKE SHE'S TWELVE YEARS OLD, AND THE FREAKS IN THE AUDIENCE ARE LAPPING IT UP.

I FIND MYSELF WISHING I WAS BACK ON GRACIE STREET.

I'D BE WANTING TO TAKE A SHOWER AFTER THAT.

CAN I TALK TO YOU FOR A MOMENT?

SURE. WHAT'S IT ABOUT?

YOU HAVE TO UNDERSTAND, I WAS NEVER REALLY INTO HER SCENE. I MEAN, I SWING BOTH WAYS, BUT I'M NOT INTO PAIN.

OR MAYBE I SHOULD SAY, MY RELATIONSHIPS ARE ALWAYS PAINFUL, BUT IT'S NOT SOMETHING I GO LOOKING FOR. IT'S NOT WHAT I WANT. IT JUST SEEMS TO HAPPEN, BUT WITH HER...

THE WHIPS AND THE PIERCINGS AND ALL THAT SHIT, IT WAS JUST TOO MUCH.

I WAIT FOR HER THE NEXT NIGHT, BUT SHE DOESN'T SHOW.

I HAVE NO REASON TO WORRY ABOUT HER, BUT I'M UNEASY.

I KEEP GOING OVER WHAT SHE TOLD ME ABOUT THIS THING.

HOW IT WAS GIVEN TO HER BY THIS FAERIE PRINCE.

HOW IT DOESN'T WORK FOR EVERYBODY, BUT WHEN IT DOES IT CAN GIVE THE PERSON WEARING IT SECOND SIGHT.

HOW IT PROTECTS THE PERSON WEARING IT FROM THE DARK SIDE OF FAERIE-THE GHOULS AND THE GOBLINS AND THE THINGS THAT GO BUMP IN THE NIGHT.

NOT THAT I BELIEVE ANY OF IT. NOT FOR A MOMENT.

BUT ALL DAY LONG I HAVEN'T BEEN ABLE TO SHAKE THE FEELING THAT SOMEBODY'S WATCHING ME.

THERE'S NO ONE THING I CAN POINT TO WITH CERTAINTY. IT'S JUST A PRICKLING SENSATION THAT I FEEL ON THE NAPE OF MY NECK. A SENSE OF MOVEMENT CAUGHT OUT OF THE CORNER OF MY EYE. A KIND OF INTUITION....

OR SECOND SIGHT?

I CAN'T WAIT FOR HER ANY LONGER. I'M GETTING THE WILLIES SITTING HERE ON MY OWN. THERE'S NO ONE IN THE BUILDING EXCEPT ME.

AND WHATEVER MIGHT BE WATCHING ME...

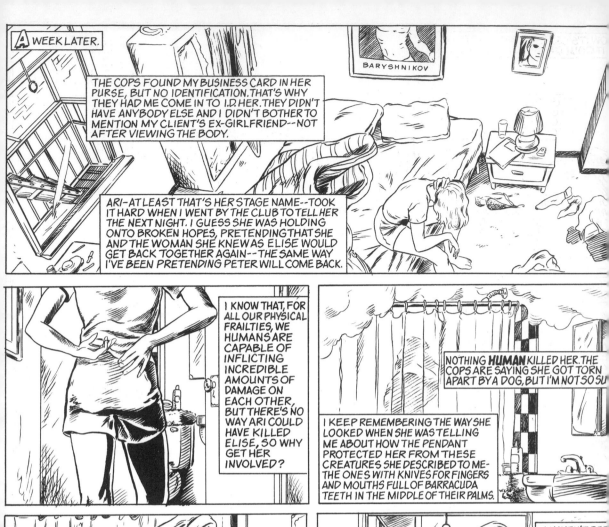

A WEEK LATER.

THE COPS FOUND MY BUSINESS CARD IN HER PURSE, BUT NO IDENTIFICATION. THAT'S WHY THEY HAD ME COME IN TO I.D. HER. THEY DIDN'T HAVE ANYBODY ELSE AND I DIDN'T BOTHER TO MENTION MY CLIENT'S EX-GIRLFRIEND--NOT AFTER VIEWING THE BODY.

ARI--AT LEAST THAT'S HER STAGE NAME--TOOK IT HARD WHEN I WENT BY THE CLUB TO TELL HER THE NEXT NIGHT. I GUESS SHE WAS HOLDING ONTO BROKEN HOPES, PRETENDING THAT SHE AND THE WOMAN SHE KNEW AS ELISE WOULD GET BACK TOGETHER AGAIN--THE SAME WAY I'VE BEEN PRETENDING PETER WILL COME BACK.

I KNOW THAT, FOR ALL OUR PHYSICAL FRAILTIES, WE HUMANS ARE CAPABLE OF INFLICTING INCREDIBLE AMOUNTS OF DAMAGE ON EACH OTHER, BUT THERE'S NO WAY ARI COULD HAVE KILLED ELISE, SO WHY GET HER INVOLVED?

NOTHING **HUMAN** KILLED HER. THE COPS ARE SAYING SHE GOT TORN APART BY A DOG, BUT I'M NOT SO SU

I KEEP REMEMBERING THE WAY SHE LOOKED WHEN SHE WAS TELLING ME ABOUT HOW THE PENDANT PROTECTED HER FROM THESE CREATURES SHE DESCRIBED TO ME-- THE ONES WITH KNIVES FOR FINGERS AND MOUTHS FULL OF BARRACUDA TEETH IN THE MIDDLE OF THEIR PALMS.

I WOULD'VE HAD NIGHTMARES ALL NIGHT, JUST THINKING ABOUT WHAT I SAW THERE IN THE MORGUE, IF I HADN'T HAD SO MUCH TO DRINK BEFORE I FINALLY DRAGGED MYSELF HOME.

I HAVEN'T BEE SOBER FOR A WEEK NOW, BECAUSE THI WAY I CAN JUST PUT IT ALL DOWN TO THE BOOZE

I USE IT AS A CRUTCH--THE SAME WAY I'VE BEEN USING CIGARETTES SINCE THAT NIGHT ELISE FIRST CAME INTO MY OFF

IF I'M DRUNK I CAN PRETEND SHE DIDN'T DIE THE WAY I CAN SO EASILY IMAGINE SHE DID, TORN APART BY SOME CREATURES FROM THE DARK SIDE OF THE BROTHERS GRIMM.

I CAN PRETEND THEY'RE NOT LOOKING FOR ME NOW.

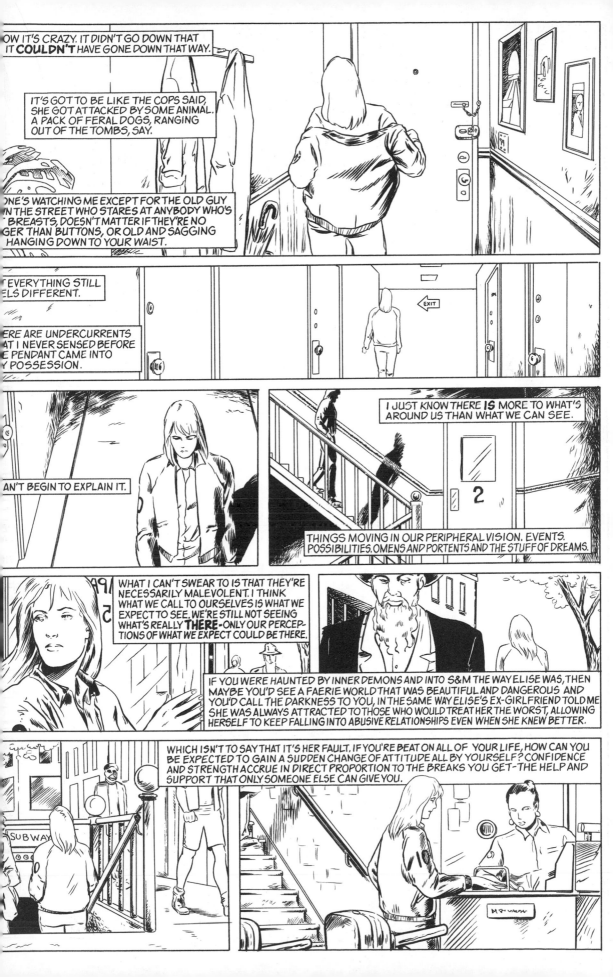

I GUESS I'M MAKING IT SOUND AS THOUGH I'VE SUDDENLY GAINED THIS HUGE BOOST OF CONFIDENCE MYSELF, BUT IN MY OWN WAY, I'M JUST AS BAD AS ARI.

SHE'S STILL SHAKING HER ASS ON STAGE AT CHIC CHEEKS, UNTOUCH BY HER CONTACT WITH THE PENDANT. SHE STILL THINKS THAT STRIP PING GIVES HER SOME KIND OF POWER OVER THE FREAKS. SHE RIGHT ON THE EDGE OF ANOTHER BAD RELATIONSHIP BECAU SHE CAN'T BREAK THE CYCLE.

AND ME? I STILL DON'T WANT TO BE ALONE. THE FOCUS OF MY LIFE IS STILL EDDYING AROUND THE FACT THAT PETER LEFT ME, THAT THERE'S SOMETHING INTRINSICALLY WRONG WITH ME, OR WHY WOULD MY RELATIONSHIPS ALWAYS FALL APART?

IT CAN'T BE JUST THAT I GET TOO INTENSE. LOVE'S **SUPPOSED** TO BE INTENSE...ISN'T IT?

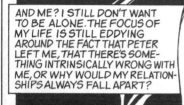

AND THEN THERE'S THIS BUSINESS WITH THE PENDANT.

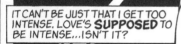

I STILL THINK SOMETHING'S WATCHING ME. OR SOME**THINGS**.

AND I DON'T KNOW IF THEY'RE STALKING ME OR SIMPLY CURIOUS.

IT'S FUNNY HOW YOUR WHOLE LIFE CAN CHANGE BECAUSE O THE SMALLEST THING. LIKE SOMEONE WALKING IN THROUG THE DOOR OF YOUR OFFICE.

EVERYTHING STILL **LOOKS** THE SAME, BUT NOW I FEEL LIKE THE MOST COMMON OBJECT HAS A SECRET HISTORY THAT MOST PEOPLE CAN'T SEE.

Saint Michaels

LOWERS

THE DIFFERENCE BETWEEN THEM AND ME IS, THEY DON'T EVEN THINK ABOUT IT.

I KNOW THIS KNOWLEDGE KILLED ELISE, BUT SOMEHOW I CAN'T BELIEVE IT'S DANGEROUS, IN AND OF ITSELF. THE REAL DANGER WOULD BE TO IGNORE IT. THE REAL DANGER WOULD BE TO SEE WHAT YOUR PRECONCEPTIONS HAVE LED YOU TO EXPECT, INSTEAD OF STRIVING TO SEE WHAT REALLY IS THERE.

I'M NOT GOING TO MAKE ELISE'S MISTAKE.

I WON'T SAY I'M NOT NERVOUS. THE IDEA OF ALL THESE...PRESENCES AROUND ME REALLY CREEPS ME OUT. BUT THEY DON'T HAVE TO BE MALEVOLENT, DO THEY? ARE HOPES ALWAYS BROKEN?

MAYBE I'M BEING A POLLYANNA. MAYBE THE WORLD REALLY IS AN UGLY PIECE OF WORK. BUT I DON'T WANT TO BELIEVE THAT. I WANT TO THINK I'M BREAKING A CYCLE.

THINK I CAN LOOK INTO THIS UNSEEN WORLD OF FAERIE E WAY THAT FRIEND OF MINE LOOKED INTO THE LESBIAN ENE. SHE TOOK FROM IT THE IMAGE OF A STRONG IDEAL,

FEELING LUCKY?

MEONE IN CONTROL OF HER OWN DESTINY, AND IT MADE R STRONGER. SHE TOOK THE IDEA OF IT--THE KNOWLEDGE AT IT CAN BE DONE--AND THAT WAS WHAT LET HER DO IT FOR HERSELF.

AND THAT'S WHAT I WANT TO DO. I WANT TO LOOK INTO FAERIE AND KNOW THAT EVERYTHING CAN BE DIFFERENT. I WANT TO BREAK THE CYCLE OF MY OLD PATTERNS. I WANT TO THROW AWAY MY CRUTCHES AND ADDICTIONS.

BUS STOP

I WANT TO STEP INTO A WORLD WHERE ANYTHING IS POS-SIBLE--WHERE I CAN BE ANYTHING OR ANYBODY.

WANT TO FIND STRENGTH IN MY SOLITUDE O THAT WHEN I DO INTERACT WITH OTHER EOPLE, I WON'T HOLD ON SO TIGHTLY WHEN HEY'RE WITH ME. SO THAT I CAN LET THEM O WHEN WE HAVE TO BE APART.

ELISE

BORN...

DIED JULY 23,
1994

R.I.P.

HER PAIN AND MINE.

THAT'D BE A KIND
OF MAGIC, TOO,
WOULDN'T IT?

R.I.P

spirit is the truth
I. John, 5:07

WE CAN'T CLOSE OUR EYES TO IT, NOT
THE MAGIC, NOT THE PAIN, BECAUSE
IF WE DO, WE MIGHT AS WELL CLOSE
THEM FOREVER.

Jesting With Chaos

It would be easier to list what *Michael Moorcock* hasn't done. He published his first novel in 1961; edited the famed *New Worlds* magazine from 1961 to 1980; has performed and written music for the rock bands *Hawkwind* and *Blue Oyster Cult*; published seventy novels; and has won the Guardian Prize, Nebula award, and the World Fantasy Award. Moorcock's *Eternal Champion* series was recently collected in 16 volumes from Millennium in the UK and White Wolf in the United States. Mojo Press will be publishing the 30th anniversary edition of Moorcock's Nebula award winning novella, *Behold The Man* in 1996.

Franz Henkel has written graphic novels/series for Kitchen Sink, Dark Horse, Marvel, Rebel and others. Current and upcoming projects include *The Exile of Abra-khan* (Marvel), *Way Of The Sorcerer* (Marvel), *Flesh Wounds* (Kitchen Sink), and *Prey For Us Sinners* (Fantaco). His first SF novel, *The Mimosa Sector* (Kaya Production), is due out in 1996.

A long time Moorcock fan, *Shea Anton Pensa* was thrilled to be the first artist to produce a fully painted Elric tale. Shea has done work on *Green Arrow* (DC), *Sandman* (DC/Vertigo), *Hammer of God* (Dark Horse), *Mondo 2000*, and *Spawn* (Image).

Ted Naifeh is a talented San Francisco based artist and former Russ Manning Award nominee for best new talent.

JESTING WITH CHAOS

by Michael Moorcock
adapted by Franz Henkel   art by Shea Anton Pensa

...AND IT WAS LEFT TO THE HORSEMAN TO FIND THE HORROR-CRAZED MAN.
AAAAHH! TESHWAN!
ELRIC OF MELNIBONE RECOGNIZED THE NAME. HE SENSED OTHER, MORE OMINOUS, DENIZENS LURKING ABOUT...
...YET HE WAS UNTROUBLED, REGARDING THEM AS ANOTHER, MORE NORMAL MAN MIGHT REGARD THE OMNI-PRESENT SONG OF BIRDS...
...THE RUSTLE OF SMALL RODENTS IN THE UNDER-GROWTH.
TESHWAN!
SHARP WHISPERINGS.
WERE THEY CARRIED ON THE AIR...
AAAAHHHNNN!
...OR WERE THEY SLITHERING ABOUT IN HIS JELLIED BRAIN?
AH!
WHO ARE YOU? AID ME! I BEG YOU, AID ME!

I WARN YOU, ELRIC -- I HAVE ONE POWER LEFT.

I CAN SEND YOU SCREAMING FROM THIS PLACE -- INTO ANOTHER. IT IS THE POWER WHICH TESHWAN GIVES ALL HIS SERVANTS.

IT IS THE ONE HE NEVER TAKES BACK!

WHY NOT SEND YOUR HUNGRY FRIENDS INTO THIS OTHER PLACE?

THEY ARE NOT HUMAN. BUT IF YOU LEAVE ME, I SHALL LAY MY LAST ENCHANTMENT UPON YOU!

YOUR LAST, PERHAPS, BUT NOT THE LAST OR THE FIRST TO BE LAID UPON ME.

NOW I MUST GO AND SEARCH FOR A QUIETER PLACE THAN THIS WHERE I CAN SLEEP UNDISTERBED.

TESHWAN -- RETURN! RETURN TO DO ME ONE LAST SERVICE -- A DEED OF VENGANCE -- A PART OF OUR BARGAIN, TESHWAN!

TESHWAN!

AAAIIIIEEEE!!!

HAHAHAHA HAHAHAHA HAHA

ELRIC RODE THROUGH THE NIGHT, NOT CARING TO SLEEP...

THIS, AT LEAST, WILL SAVE ME FROM BOREDOM.
WHO VISITS THE PALACE OF KANELOON AT THE TIME OF THE CHANGE?
A VOICE LIKE LIMBO'S MUSIC.
THE SYMBOL OF CHAOS.
YOUR MASTERS, I GATHER, KNOW ME-- FOR THEY AIDED THEIR SERVANT SLORG IN SENDING ME HITHER.
BUT TELL THEM IT IS ELRIC OF MELNIBONE, NONETHELESS-- ELRIC, DESTROYER OF DREAMING IMRRYR. KINSLAYER AND OUTCAST. THEY WILL KNOW ME.
MY MASTERS ORDER ME TO INFORM YOU THAT YOU MAY ENTER BUT THAT, HAVING ONCE COME TO THE PALACE OF KANELOON, YOU MAY NEVER LEAVE SAVE UNDER CERTAIN CONDITIONS.
THOSE CONDITIONS?
OF THESE THEY WILL TELL YOU IF YOU ENTER. ARE YOU RECKLESS-- OR WILL YOU STAND PONDERING?
I'LL AVAIL MYSELF OF THEIR GENEROSITY.

GREETINGS TO YOU, MORTAL. YOU ARE THE FIRST FOR SOME TIME TO SIT WITH THE LORDS OF CHAOS AT THE TIME OF THE CHANGE.

BEHOLD,-- THERE ARE OTHERS WHO HAVE HAD THE PRIVILEGE.

THEY WERE STILL ALIVE...

I WOULD NOT BE SO IMPERTINENT, MY LORDS, AS TO SET MYSELF BESIDE YOU ALL INSOFAR AS POWERS ARE CONCERNED, BUT YOU KNOW THAT I AM ELRIC OF MELNIBONE AND THAT MY RACE IS OLD.

MY DEFICIENT BLOOD IS THE ROYAL BLOOD OF THE KINGS OF THE DREAMING CITY.

I DO NOT KNOW WHAT YOU REQUIRE OF ME, AND I THANK YOU FOR YOUR HOSPITALITY NONETHELESS, BUT I BELIEVE THAT I CAN CONDUCT MYSELF BETTER IN MOST WAYS THAN CAN ANY OTHER MORTAL.

NOW, KNOW YOU THAT I BE TESHWAN, AND THESE NEED NOT BE NAMED AND MAY BE ADDRESSED SINGLY OR COLLECTIVELY BY THE NAME OF LORDS OF CHAOS.

COME, SIT HERE BESIDE ME AND I WILL INFORM YOU OF WHAT WE EXPECT.

YOU ARE MORE FAVORED THAN OTHERS HAVE BEEN, ELRIC, AND, IN TRUTH, I WELCOMED THE OPPORTUNITY GIVEN ME BY MY VENGEFUL SERVANT SLORG BEFORE HE DIED.

LET US HOPE SO, ELRIC OF MELNIBONÉ, FOR WE WOULD NOT WISH YOU TO FAIL, KNOW THAT. BESIDES, YOU ARE NOT FULLY MORTAL AS HUMANS UNDERSTAND THE WORD.

LORD TESHWAN-- MY LORDS OF CHAOS.

NOW, HERE'S THE SITUATION IN WHICH WE HAVE DECIDED TO PLACE YOU.

YOU MAY LEAVE ONLY IF YOU CAN CREATE SOMETHING WHICH IT HAS NEVER OCCURRED TO US TO CREATE.

BUT YOU, SURELY, ARE THE MASTERS OF CREATION? HOW MAY I DO THIS?

YOUR FIRST STATEMENT IS NOT STRICTLY TRUE AND IN QUALIFYING IT I CAN GIVE YOU A HINT OF THE ANSWER TO YOUR QUESTION.

WE OF CHAOS CANNOT MAKE ANYTHING NEW-- WE MAY ONLY EXPERIMENT WITH COMBINATIONS OF THAT WHICH WAS ALREADY CREATED.

DO YOU UNDERSTAND?

I DO.

FOR LONG HOURS THE PAGEANT OF CHAOS CONTINUED AS THE LORDS TOOK THE ELEMENTS OF HIS WORLD AND SHOOK THEM ABOUT, TURNED THEM INSIDE OUT, STOOD THEM ON END...

...MADE STARTLING, STRANGE, BEAUTIFUL UNHOLY COMBINATIONS UNTIL THEY WERE SATISFIED WITH THE CONSTANT MOVEMENT OF THE SCENE ABOUT THEM, THE PERPETUAL SHIFTING AND CHANGING.

THEY HAD SET A PATTERN THAT WAS
NO PATTERN, WHICH WOULD LAST
UNTIL THEY BECAME BORED WITH
THEIR DOMAIN AGAIN AND BROUGHT
ABOUT ANOTHER TIME OF THE CHANGE.

THIS IS SPLENDID IMPERTINENCE, I GRANT YOU-- BUT THIS IS NOTHING NEW-- YOU ALREADY SIT THERE BESIDE US.

INDEED. BUT LOOK IN THE MAN'S MIND.

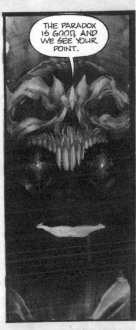

THE PARADOX IS GOOD, AND WE SEE YOUR POINT.

WE HAVE, FOR AN ETERNITY, CREATED THE EFFECT. YOU, IN YOUR PRIDE AND INNOCENCE, HAVE CREATED THE CAUSE.

IN THAT MAN'S MIND WAS ALL THAT COULD EVER EXIST.

YOU HAVE NOTED THE PARADOX?

Dinosaur Love

Better known as an editor, *Richard Klaw* has had two stories appear in JAB (Adhesive) as well as the publication of the first issue of his series *Wings: Learning To Fly* (MU Press). Future projects include *Dain Bramage* (an issue of Aeon Focus), a new story in *JAB*, and a graphic novel from Mojo.

Newt Manwich's work will appear in *JAB* (Adhesive), *Punk Origin Special* (CFD), and *Dain Bramage*. This is his first professionally published story.

Little Johnny Lovecloud is currently on death row in a Texas prison. He maintains his innocence, saying that the pistol he was cleaning in the bank accidentally went off eight times.

Michael Washburn's work has appeared in *Shottloose* (Absolute) and *JAB* (Adhesive).

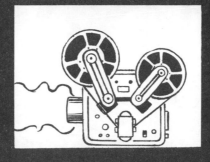

IN THE 1950'S MIGHTY WEAPONS WERE UNLEASHED, AWAKENING TERRIFYING MONSTERS FROM PREHISTORIC EARTH. THE **DINOSAUR** WAS BACK.

BUT WITH SOME SKILL...

...A LITTLE LUCK...

...AND A LOT OF BIG GUNS...

...THE DINOSAUR WAS RETURNED TO THE EXTINCTION FROM WHICH IT CAME.

OR SO THEY THOUGHT.

From the journals of Dr. Thaddeus Martin:

My experiments are almost complete as I am prepared to connect the brain. All I need is lightning and the name of Dr. Thaddeus Martin will be revered as the greatest mind this planet has ever known!

Eventually I was able to install the brain. Apparently the brain excretes abnormal amounts of pheromones, which would explain the deviant behavior.

I wonder what effect this brain will have on my creation. What effect will it have on others?

AT LAST!

I WILL PREPARE THE LABORATORY. YOU TAKE CARE OF THE INTERLOPERS.

BLAM!

KRAKABOOM!

GONNA HAVE TO CUT THE SLEEVE.

FUCKING BRAIN! NOTHING BUT BAD NEWS SINCE WE GOT IT.

WE KNEW THERE WAS SOMETHING ODD FROM THE MOMENT WE GOT THERE. I NEVER WANTED TO FUCK A CORPSE, BUT I WAS SORELY TEMPTED.

AFTER ALL SHE WAS MARILYN MONROE. EVEN DEAD SHE HAD THE POWER TO MANIPULATE. TO MAKE MEN DO THINGS. THAT'S WHY THEY HAD HER KILLED.

THAT'S WHY WE NEEDED THE BRAIN. TO KEEP IT AWAY FROM THEM. TO STOP THEM FROM HARNESSING THE POWER.

WE WERE FOOLS. NO ONE CAN CONTROL THAT. WE WERE LUCKY TO SURVIVE WITH OUR SANITY.

SOMEHOW WE MANAGED TO CONTAIN THE BRAIN. WE DEDICATED OUR LIVES TO SAFEGUARDING SOCIETY FROM THE POWER OF MARILYN MONROE'S BRAIN!

IT WAS UNEVENTFUL UNTIL NOW. SOME PENCIL NECK STOLE THE BRAIN FOR HIS OWN NEFARIOUS PURPOSE. WE MUST GET HER BACK!

KRACKABOOM!

KRACKABOOM!

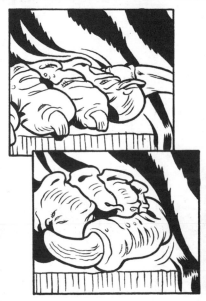

YES!

GOOD WORK IGOR. HOLD THEM UNTIL I GET THERE.

I'LL BE RIGHT BACK.

WHAT MARTIN SAID EARLIER. WAS HE TELLING THE TRUTH?

THEN LET'S DO IT.

SPLASH!

A FRIEND ONCE TOLD ME THAT TRUE LOVE WAS WORTH MORE THAN GOOD FRIENDSHIP. WITH THAT IN MIND I HAVE NO REGRETS.

I HAVE THE LOVE OF MARILYN MONROE, FREEDOM, AND A WORLD TO EXPLORE. SO WHAT IF I'M A 30 FOOT TALL MONSTER.

HEY, THAT'S THE WAY IT IS WITH DINOSAUR LOVE.

I JUST HOPE IGOR TAKES CARE OF MY BODY. I MIGHT NEED IT BACK.

THE END

Masque Of The Red Death

As they say, this is a man who needs no introduction. *Edgar Allan Poe* is one of the prominent figures in literature. Although he was respected as a literary critic, his short stories and poems were neglected until publication of *The Raven and Other Poems* in 1845. Poe died in 1849, leaving behind a legacy of great literature.

Eric Burnham adapted Grant Morrison's "Braille Encyclopedia" for *Verotika* (Verotik). He currently lives in the San Francisco Bay area.

Though not as famous as Edgar Allan Poe, *Ted Naifeh* has established himself as a talented newcomer in comics with his work on *The Machine* (Dark Horse), *Medal Of Honor* (Dark Horse), *Verotika* (Verotik), *Creature Features* (Mojo), and *Underground* (Dark Horse). Ted is the artist for the upcoming *Exile Of Abra-khan* (Marvel) and the second *Lone Ranger & Tonto* mini-series (Topps).

One of the best kept secrets in comics, *Martin Thomas* has colored books for DC, Marvel, First, Viz, and others. His prominent work includes *Grimjack* (First), *Crying Freeman* (Viz), and the covers to Shannon Wheeler's *Too Much Coffee Man* (Adhesive). He is hard at work on *Big Justice* (Adhesive), which he writes, inks, and colors.

The Masque of the Red Death

by
Edgar A. Poe
adapted by Eric Burnham
art by Ted Naifeh
color by Martin Thomas

THE RED DEATH HAD LONG DEVASTATED THE COUNTRY.

NO PESTILENCE HAD EVER BEEN SO FATAL, OR SO HIDEOUS.

THE COUNTRYSIDE WAS RAVAGED. CITIES, TOWNS AND VILLAGES FELL QUICKLY INTO A STATE OF DEPOPULATION.

AND EVERYWHERE, THOSE WHO REMAINED ALIVE SOUGHT SOME HOPE FOR PLACE OF SANCTUARY.

THE WHOLE SEIZURE, PROGRESS AND TERMINATION OF THE DISEASE, WERE THE INCIDENTS OF BUT HALF AN HOUR.

THERE WERE SHARP PAINS, AND SUDDEN DIZZINESS, AND THEN PROFUSE BLEEDING AT THE PORES, WITH DISSOLUTION.

THESE SCARLET STAINS UPON THE BODY AND FACE MARKED THE VICTIM.

GRACIOUS LORD IN HEAVEN, WHERE IS THERE MERCY FROM THIS PESTILENCE?!

AND THUS MARKED, HE WAS SHUT OUT FROM THE AID AND SYMPATHY OF HIS FELLOW-MEN.

BUT NOT ALL MEN WERE BORN TO SUFFER. DESPITE THE DREARY FATE OF HIS DOMINION, PRINCE PROSPERO WAS HAPPY AND DAUNTLESS AND SAGACIOUS.

HE FOUGHT DESPAIR WITH A LIGHT HEARTED MANNER, AND SUMMONED TO HIS COMPANY A THOUSAND HALE AND HEARTY FRIENDS FROM HIS COURT WHO SHARED A SIMILAR MIND.

THEY THEN RETIRED TO THE DEEP SECLUSION OF ONE OF HIS CASTELLATED ABBEYS.

THERE TO WAIT OUT THE DEVASTATION IN GOOD SPIRITS AND PLEASANT REVELRY.

THE STRUCTURE WAS SOLID, A STRONG AND LOFTY WALL GIRDLED IT, AND THIS WALL HAD GATES OF IRON.

ONCE ENTERED, NONE COULD DEPART. THIS WAS TO ASSURE THAT NOTHING UNWELCOME COULD JOIN THEM.

BY HAMMER AND FURNACE, THE LOCKS AND BOLTS WERE MADE SECURE. IT WAS AN IMPREGNABLE GATE.

CEASE YOUR MOCKING WORDS. IT IS A PROPER THING THAT THE PRINCE FINDS JOY IN OUR SALVATION.

TOWARD THE FIFTH OR SIXTH MONTH OF SECLUSION, PRINCE PROSPERO ENTERTAINED HIS THOUSAND FRIENDS AT A MASKED BALL OF THE MOST UNUSUAL MAGNIFICENCE.

IT WAS A VOLUPTUOUS SCENE, THAT MASQUERADE. AH, BUT FIRST YOU MUST HEAR OF THE ROOMS IN WHICH IT WAS HELD.

THERE WERE SEVEN, MAKING AN IMPERIAL SUITE, BUT CRAFTED IN AN UNUSUAL FASHION. A SHARP TURN OCCURRED EVERY TWENTY OR THIRTY YARDS SO THAT AT NO POINT COULD A GUEST VIEW MORE THAN A SINGLE CHAMBER.

THE APARTMENTS WERE LIGHTED EACH BY TWO TALL AND NARROW GOTHIC WINDOWS OF STAINED GLASS ON EITHER WALL. A FLAMING BRAZIER IN A SMALL CHAMBER BEYOND CAST THE ONLY ILLUMINATION.

ALL FURNISHINGS AND TRAPPINGS OF EACH ROOM MATCHED THE COLOR OF THE STAINED GLASS AND THUS THE PROJECTED RAYS THAT FILLED IT. THE EASTERN MOST WAS DONE IN BLUE, THE SECOND WAS PURPLE.

THE THIRD WAS GREEN THROUGHOUT, AND SO WERE THE CASEMENTS. THE FOURTH WAS CURTAINED AND LIGHTED WITH ORANGE, THE FIFTH IN WHITE, THE SIXTH IN VIOLET.

ALL THIS CAME AS NO SURPRISE TO THE PRINCE'S GUESTS WHO HAD BECOME ACCUSTOMED TO HIS LOVE OF THE BIZARRE.

BUT TO ACCEPT SUCH THINGS COMPLETELY IS ANOTHER THING. THE SEVENTH AND FINAL CHAMBER WAS DECORATED ENTIRELY IN BLACK, WITH VELVET TAPESTRIES AND THICK CARPET.

BUT UNLIKE THE OTHERS, THE WINDOWS OF THIS ROOM DID NOT CORRESPOND. ITS PANES WERE COLOURED A DEEP, SCARLET RED.

IT WAS IN THIS APARTMENT, ALSO, THAT THERE STOOD AGAINST THE WESTERN WALL, A GIGANTIC CLOCK OF EBONY.

THIS PRODUCED AN EFFECT WHICH WAS GHASTLY IN THE EXTREME. FEW OF THE COMPANY WERE BOLD ENOUGH TO TARRY LONG WITHIN, OR EVEN TO ENTER AT ALL.

ITS PENDULUM SWUNG TO AND FRO WITH A DULL, HEAVY, MONOTONOUS CLANG.

WHEN THE MINUTE-HAND MADE THE CIRCUIT OF THE FACE, AND THE HOUR WAS TO BE STRICKEN, THERE CAME FROM THE BRAZEN LUNGS OF THE CLOCK A MOST PECULIAR NOTE.

LOUD AND LONG AND DEEP.

AT EACH LAPSE OF AN HOUR, THE GATHERED HOST WOULD PAUSE AND HEARKEN TO THE SOUND. THE ORCHESTRA QUIETED, THE DANCERS STOPPED, AND THE CLOWNS FELL SILENT AND SOMBER.

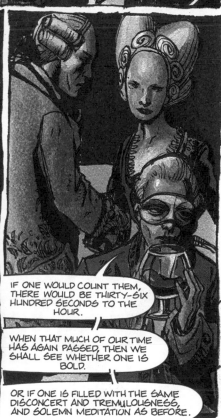

WHY MUST THAT HELLISH THING BE ALLOWED TO CHIME ITS AWFUL BELL?

PAY IT NO HEED, IT BUT PERFORMS ITS FUNCTION TO TOLL THE HOUR.

THOUGH I CONFESS, IT UNNERVES ME AS WELL.

THERE, THE TOLLING HAS STOPPED.

AND HERE I DO RESOLVE, GOOD LADY, THAT IN THE NEXT PASSING OF THE HOUR, I SHALL BE A ROCK. RESOLUTE, THAT YOU MIGHT TAKE COMFORT FROM ME.

IF ONE WOULD COUNT THEM, THERE WOULD BE THIRTY-SIX HUNDRED SECONDS TO THE HOUR.

WHEN THAT MUCH OF OUR TIME HAS AGAIN PASSED, THEN WE SHALL SEE WHETHER ONE IS BOLD.

OR IF ONE IS FILLED WITH THE SAME DISCONCERT AND TREMULOUSNESS, AND SOLEMN MEDITATION AS BEFORE.

IN SPITE OF SUCH THINGS, IT WAS A GAY AND MAGNIFICENT REVEL. AND THE COMPANY HAD PRINCE PROSPERO TO THANK.

OF THE PRINCE HIMSELF SO MUCH HAS ALREADY BEEN SUGGESTED. 'TWAS HE WHO DIRECTED THE ODD ARRANGEMENTS OF THE CHAMBER AND THE MANNER AND ATTIRE OF THE MASQUE.

HIS WAS A LUSTY SOUL THAT REVERED LIFE, AND DRANK FULL FROM THAT CUP.

HO, FAIR COMPANIONS! WE ARE ALL WELL-MET HERE. LET THE WINE FLOW AND THE ACROBATS LEAP AND THE MUSICIANS PLAY TO A MORE FERVID PACE.

LET ALL WITHIN SHARE OF OUR HAPPY ATMOSPHERE. LET NO ONE SHROUD OUR HEARTS WITH GLOOM.

SING! DANCE! PLAY!

REJOICE IN OUR BLESSED SANCTUARY!

TRUE, HIS FANCIES DISREGARDED THE DECORA OF TYPICAL FASHION, WHAT SOME MIGHT REGARD GOOD TASTE. BUT HIS PLANS WERE BOLD AND FIERY, AND HIS CONCEPTIONS GLOWED WITH A BARBARIC LUSTRE.

CLAP CLAP CLAP CLAP

AH, FILL MY CUP AGAIN LAD.

HURRAY FOR THE PRINCE!

HEAR HEAR!

THREE CHEERS!

THUS DID THE MASQUERADE CONTINUE.

THE MASKS AND COSTUMES OF THE BALL WERE OF A MOST UNUSUAL STYLE.

BE SURE THAT THEY WERE GROTESQUE.

THERE WAS MUCH GLITTER AND GLARE AND PIQUANCY AND PHANTASM.

THERE WERE ARABESQUE FIGURES WITH UNSUITED LIMBS AND APPOINTMENTS.

THERE WERE DELIRIOUS AND MADMAN FASHIONS.

THERE WAS MUCH OF THE BEAUTIFUL AND MUCH OF THE WANTON.

THERE WALKED AND WRITHED AND GLIDED THROUGH THOSE HALLS A MULTITUDE OF DREAMS.

DREAMS WHICH TOOK, PERHAPS, GRUSOME FORM, BUT PULSED WITH THE FEVERISH BEAT OF LIFE.

THERE WERE ALL THESE THINGS, SOME OF THEM TERRIBLE, AND SOME MEANT TO INSPIRE A LITTLE DISGUST.

IN SUCH AN ASSEMBLY OF FREAKISH PHANTASMS, IT COULD BE ASSUMED THAT NO ORDINARY APPEARANCE COULD EXCITE MUCH SENSATION.

IT WAS BRIEFLY BEFORE THE MIDNIGHT HOUR THAT MANY IN THE CROWD HAD FOUND LEISURE TO BECOME AWARE OF A MASKED FIGURE UNNOTICED BEFORE.

NOW EVEN WITH SUCH RECKLESS SORTS, TO WHOM LIFE AND DEATH WERE EQUAL JESTS, THERE ARE MATTERS OF WHICH NO JEST CAN BE MADE.

INDEED, THE WHOLE COMPANY SEEMED NOW DEEPLY TO FEEL THAT IN THE COSTUME AND BEARING OF THE STRANGER, NEITHER WIT NOR PROPRIETY EXISTED.

WE HERE HAVE GATHERED TO CELEBRATE OUR CONQUERING OF DEATH! WE HAVE TAKEN GARB AND MANNER TO HONOR THE POWER AND DARKNESS OF THE OUTSIDE.

BLASPHEMY... I SAY IT IS A BLASPHEMY!

HOW... HOW DARE...

TO HONOR AND ACKNOWLEDGE OUR PASSING FROM IT!

BUT YOU! YOU COULD NOT BE SATISFIED WITH THESE OFFERED FASHIONS!

HOW DARE YOU!!

YOUR GARMENTS BEAR THE VERY SIGN OF THE PESTILENCE OUTSIDE.

DEAR GOD, HOW FAR HAVE YOU GONE TO MAINTAIN THIS GRUESOME ROLE? IS THIS TRUE BLOOD I SEE STAINING YOUR TORN ROBES?

AND THEN THAT GREAT AND TERRIBLE CLOCK TOLLED THE FINAL CHIME OF MIDNIGHT.

WOULD YOU TEMPT GOD AND SATAN? IS IT PLEASING TO YOU TO BRING THIS RED DEATH TO OUR MASQUERADE?

WHAT HAS HAPPENED HERE?

HE HAS SLAIN THE PRINCE! OUR GOOD PRINCE IS DEAD!

HE MUST BE MADE TO PAY! WE MUST KILL HIM!

THERE IS NOTHING HERE. NOTHING TO FEAR.

BUT BID OUR MASTER AWAKEN. HE CANNOT HAVE BEEN SLAIN BY A PHANTOM.

HE SPEAKS TRUTH! THESE ARE BUT EMPTY ROBES.

BUT WHAT OF THIS...?

AND NOW WAS ACKNOWLEDGED THE PRESENCE OF THE RED DEATH. HE HAD COME LIKE A THIEF IN THE NIGHT.

AND THE REVELERS KNEW THAT ONE BY ONE THEY WOULD DROP AWAY, EACH IN THE DESPAIRING POSTURE OF HIS FALL.

BUT THIS CERTAIN KNOWLEDGE DID NOT STOP THEM FROM SEEKING TO ESCAPE THEIR FATE.

THOUGH THE WALLS WERE SOLID, THE DOORS MAINLY FIRM, AND THAT GREAT, MASSIVE GATE.

AND THE LIFE OF THE EBONY CLOCK WENT OUT AND THE FLAMES OF THE BRAZIERS EXPIRED.

AND DARKNESS AND DECAY AND THE RED DEATH HELD ILLIMITABLE DOMINION OVER ALL.

Real Thing

Nancy A. Collins' first novel, *Sunglasses After Dark*, is one of the best vampire novels of the 80's and won both the Bram Stoker and British Fantasy Awards. Since then Nancy has written three other novels (one featuring Sonja Blue, the heroine of Sunglasses), a run of *Swamp Thing* (DC/Vertigo), and loads of short stories. Upcoming works include *Midnight Blue*, a Sonja Blue omnibus with *Paint It Black*, the third Sonja Blue book; as well as a *Sunglasses After Dark* comic series for Verotik.

Morgan has painted covers for *Modern Perversity* (Blackbird), *Wings: Learning To Fly* (MU Press), and *JAB* (Adhesive). His black & white painted interior work has appeared in *Creature Features* (Mojo) and *Modern Perversity*. Morgan currently lives in Austin, Texas, where he does artwork for computer games.

THE RED RAVEN'S A REAL PIT. THE JOHNS ARE ALWAYS BACKING UP AND THE PLACE SMELLS OF RANK PISS AND STALE BEER. DURING THE WEEK IT'S JUST ANOTHER NEIGHBORHOOD DIVE, SERVING TRUCK DRIVERS AND BARFLIES. NOT A BUKOWSKI AMONGST THEM.

STILL, THE DRINKS ARE CHEAP AND THE BARTENDERS RARELY ASK TO SEE I.D., SO ON THE WEEKENDS THE CLIENTELE CHANGES RADICALLY, GROWING YOUNGER AND STRANGER. STILL NOT A BUKOWSKI AMONGST THEM.

NORMALLY I DON'T BOTHER WITH JOINTS LIKE THIS. BUT I'VE BEEN HEARING ABOUT A BLOOD CULT OPERATING OUT OF THE RED RAVEN.

I MAKE IT MY BUSINESS TO ALWAYS CHECK OUT RUMORS. MOST TIMES IT'S NOTHING BUT GAS-- BUT OCCASIONALLY THERE'S SOMETHING MORE SINISTER BEHIND THEM.

FINDING OUT WHAT'S GOING DOWN ISN'T THAT HARD, REALLY. ALL I'VE GOT TO DO IS KEEP MY EARS OPEN AND LISTEN...

-OF THE UNDEAD. HE'S THE REAL THING-

C'MON, GUYS-- A *REAL* VAMPIRE?

HIS NAME IS RHYMER. LORD RHYMER. HE'S THREE HUNDRED YEARS OLD.

-TOLD HIM HE COULD KISS MY ASS GOODBYE-

-REALLY LIKED THEIR LAST ALBUM-

-BITCH ACTED LIKE I'D DONE SOMETHING-

-UNTIL NEXT PAYDAY. I PROMISE YOU'LL GET IT-

THERE. THAT ONE.

WE TOLD HIM ABOUT YOU, SHAWNA. HE SAID HE WANTED TO MEET YOU.

REALLY?

I SEEM TO HAVE FOUND WHAT I WAS LOOKING FOR. BUT SOME-THING DOESN'T FEEL QUITE RIGHT...

VAMPIRES USUALLY AVOID GOTHS LIKE THE PLAGUE. THEIR ADOLESCENT FASCINATION WITH DEATH AND EXTRAVAGANT FASHION SENSE CALLS FAR TOO MUCH ATTENTION TO THEMSELVES. VAMPIRES PREFER THEIR VICTIM TO BE MORE NONDESCRIPT... THEIR SERVANTS MORE DISCRETE...

THEIR LAIR LESS OBVIOUS...

THERE'S SOMETHING NOT RIGHT ABOUT THIS. I JUST CAN'T FIGURE OUT **WHAT**...

IF I WANT TO KNOW WHAT'S GOING DOWN HERE, I BETTER GET INSIDE. I WON'T LEARN ANYTHING HANGING AROUND OUTSIDE, THAT MUCH IS CERTAIN...

DOESN'T LOOK LIKE I'VE MISSED ANY-THING...

L-LORD RHYMER?

YES, SERGE? WHAT IS IT?

The Real Thing
Story: NANCY A. COLLINS
Art: MORGAN
Letters: BRAD THOMTE

SONYA BLUE Created by
NANCY A. COLLINS

I DON'T LIKE THIS. I DON'T LIKE THIS ONE LITTLE BIT... BUT NOW IS NOT THE TIME TO DO ANYTHING ABOUT IT.

COME TO ME, MY BRIDE...

THAT'S IT, MY DEAR. COME TO ME AS YOU HAVE DREAMED OF SO MANY, MANY TIMES BEFORE.

Nnnnn!

IT IS DONE. YOU ARE NOW BOUND TO ME BY THE STRENGTH OF MY IMMORTAL WILL.

I THOUGHT THOSE LOSERS WERE *NEVER* GOING TO LEAVE.

NOW'S THE TIME TO PAY A SOCIAL CALL ON THEIR SO-CALLED "MASTER". HOPE HE'S IN THE MOOD FOR A LITTLE CHAT BEFORE BEDDY-BYE.

YAAAAWN!

WHAT--? WHO'S THERE?

OKAY, BUDDY, WHAT THE HELL ARE YOU TRYING TO PULL HERE--?

Hsssss!

CAN THE ACT, ASSHOLE! YOU'RE NOT FOOLING ME FOR ONE SECOND!

ONLY HUMANS THINK VAMPIRES NEED TO SLEEP ON A LAYER OF THEIR HOME SOIL.

BUDDY, I KNEW DRACULA-- AND BELIEVE ME, YOU'RE NO DRACULA.

Oooof!

JUST WHAT I THOUGHT: CUSTOM-MADE DENTURES. AND THE EYES ARE CONTACT LENSES, RIGHT? AND I BET THE NAILS ARE LEE PRESS-ONS, TOO...

HAT THE FUCK E YOU PLAYING HERE, JERK? 'E YOU RUNNING ME KIND OF SCAM THESE GOTH KIDS?

I'M NOT A CON-MAN, IF THAT'S WHAT Y-YOU'RE THINKING. I-I'M NOT DOING IT FOR MONEY...

"A-ALL M-MY LIFE I'VE BEEN AN OUTSIDER. N-NO ONE EVER PAID ANY ATTENTION TO ME. N-NOT EVEN M-MY OWN PARENTS. N-NO ONE EVER TOOK ME S-SERIOUSLY.

BRIDES OF DRACULA

YOU'RE A VAMPIRE! A *REAL* VAMPIRE!

P-PLEASE! *PLEEEASE!* M-MAKE ME ONE OF YOU!

I WAS AFRAID THIS WAS GOING TO HAPPEN.

I'LL DO ANYTHING YOU WANT-- GIVE YOU ANYTHING YOU NEED! JUST MAKE ME LIKE YOU!

B-BITE ME! DRINK MY B-BLOOD!

EVEN KNOWING THAT THIS WAS BOUND TO HAPPEN, I CAN'T HELP BUT FEEL...OVERWHELM-ED BY DISGUST.

I LOOK AT THIS PIECE OF HUMAN FLOTSAM AND SEE AN ASSHOLE SO ALIENATED, SO STUNTED, THAT HIS DRIVING DREAM IS TO BE A WALKING DEADMAN. AND I START TO REMEMBER...

I REMEMBER HOW A SIXTEEN-YEAR-OLD GIRL NAMED DENISE THORNE WAS SEDUCED BY A SMOOTH-TALK-ING STRANGER WHO CALLED HIMSELF LORD MORGAN ——ONLY TO BE RAVAGED BY A BLOOD-EYED DEMON THAT HID BEHIND HIS FACE...

HOW HER NAKED, ABUSED BODY WAS THROWN INTO THE GUTTER AND LEFT FOR DEAD...

BUT SHE WAS FAR FROM DEAD. SHE WAS ME.

YOU WANT TO BE LIKE ME?

I DON'T WANT TO BE LIKE ME!

YAAAAR!

NO! Arrg—*

I GUESS I LOST IT FOR A MINUTE.

MAN, WHAT A MESS. GLAD I'M NOT THE ONE WHO HAS TO CLEAN IT UP.

THIS ISN'T THE FIRST VAMPIRE-WANNA-BE I'VE RUN INTO, BUT I'VE GOT TO ADMIT, HE HAD THE BEST SCAM. THE GOTHS WANTED THE REAL THING AND HE GAVE THEM WHAT THEY THOUGHT THEY WANTED.

POOR STUPID BASTARDS.

SO MANY HUMANS ARE FASCINATED BY THE ROMANTIC "IDEAL" OF THE VAMPIRE LOVER. TO THEM ITS ALL BLACK LEATHER, CHROME JEWELRY AND LOVE BITES, WHERE EVERY-ONE IS ETERNALLY YOUNG AND BEAUTI-FUL AND NO ONE CAN EVER HURT YOU AGAIN.

LIKE HELL.

I'M THE REAL THING, ALRIGHT. BIG AS LIFE AND TWICE AS UGLY. AND THE ONLY PLEASURE IN MY EXIST-ANCE IS TO KILL VAMPIRES...

AND THINGS THAT WANT TO BE VAMPIRES.

TONIGHT WAS A BUST, AS FAR AS I'M CONCERNED. WHEN I GO OUT HUNT- ING, I PREFER BRINGING DOWN AC- TUAL GAME, NOT *FAUX* PREDATORS...

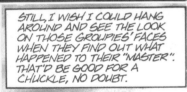

STILL, I WISH I COULD HANG AROUND AND SEE THE LOOK ON THOSE GROUPIES' FACES WHEN THEY FIND OUT WHAT HAPPENED TO THEIR "MASTER". THAT'D BE GOOD FOR A CHUCKLE, NO DOUBT.

NO ONE CAN SAY I DON'T HAVE A SENSE OF HUMOR.

Franklin & The Can Of Whup-Ass

Bill Crider is best known for his series of novels about Sheriff Dan Rhodes, who presided over a small Texas town. He's also written westerns and other weird little pieces like the one that follows.

Tom Foxmarnick cut his funnybook babyteeth writing and drawing CarToons magazine from 1980 to 1991. His work can also be found in the horror comics *Taboo* (Tundra) and *System Shock* (Tuscany Press).

FRANKLIN AND THE CAN OF

WRITTEN BY—BILL CRIDER • ART BY—TOM FOXMARNICK

3.

4.

5

FRANKLIN DECIDED TO TAKE THE LONG WAY HOME. HE DIDN'T WANT TO MEET ANYONE THAT MIGHT KNOW WHO HE WAS.

HE FOUND HIMSELF IN NEIGHBORHOODS WHERE HE'D NEVER BEEN BEFORE...

...AND WHERE HE WAS SORRY HE'D GONE...

FRANKLIN COULD SEE THAT THE TWO CARS WERE GOING TO COLLIDE IF SOMEONE DIDN'T DO SOMETHING!

7

ORDINARILY FRANKLIN WOULD NEVER HAVE SPOKEN TO A STRANGER, BUT HE KNEW THAT THIS WAS ONE MAN HE HAD TO TALK TO.

UH, MR., UHH, TIBBEDEAUX?

WHAT YOU WANT, BOY?

FRANKLIN COULDN'T REALLY SAY EXACTLY WHAT HE WANTED. HE WANTED TO TELL ABOUT HOW BEN PENNY HAD MADE HIM FEEL. ABOUT HOW HE'D HAD HIS ASS WHIPPED IN THE PARKING LOT, AND ABOUT HOW HE WANTED MORE THAN ANYTHING A WAY TO FIGHT BACK. AND HOW HE'D SEEN A RUNTY LITTLE BLACK MAN THAT COULDN'T BREAK A TOOTHPICK BACK DOWN A WHITE GIANT WITH NOTHING MORE THAN A LITTLE CAN. HE MUST HAVE STAMMERED OUT SOME OF IT BECAUSE EZRA TIBBEDEAUX SMILED.

SON, THAT MAN WASN'T SCARED OF ME. HE SCARED OF THAT CAN OF WHUP-ASS. YOU TRYIN' TO TELL ME YOU LIKE TO HAVE A CAN OF THAT TO CARRY AROUND?

UH, YES, I UH, GUESS I... UHH, DO.

I DON'T GENERALLY SELL MY WHUP-ASS. AIN'T NEVER EVEN USED IT MYSELF BUT JUST A FEW TIMES. BOY LIKE YOU SURELY NEEDS A CAN IF ANYBODY DOES, THOUGH. YOU GOT ANY MONEY, SON?

I COULD GET ABOUT, UH, TWENTY DOLLARS.

I TELL YOU WHAT. YOU COME BY MY STORE TONIGHT, 'ROUND ABOUT MIDNIGHT. YOU GOT TO SEE WHAT YOU GETTIN' 'FORE YOU BUY! WHUP-ASS AIN'T SOMETHIN' YOU BUY LIGHTLY. NOW YOU LISTEN AND I TELL YOU HOW TO GET TO MY STORE.

FRANKLIN WASN'T SURE HE COULD SNEAK AWAY FROM HIS HOUSE AT MIDNIGHT, AND HE WASN'T SURE HE COULD FIND EZRA TIBBEDEAUX'S STORE.

VRRmmm...

BUT HE KNEW ONE THING: HE KNEW HE WAS GOING TO TRY!

9.

FINALLY FRANKLIN GOT TO EZRA'S SHOP. HE COULD HARDLY BELIEVE WHAT HE SAW IN THE WINDOW. HE WANTED TO TURN AROUND AND RUN ALL THE WAY HOME.

·SPICES·
·HERBS·
TAXIDERMY

EZRA'S

BONE DUST·
SKULLS
EXOTICS

$5.00

BUT HE THOUGHT ABOUT THE WAY THE BIG WHITE MAN'S FACE HAD LOOKED WHEN HE SAW THE CAN OF WHUP-ASS...

...HE KNEW HE HAD TO GO INSIDE.

COME ON IN, BOY.

FISH
CHIC

FOLLOW ME, BOY. WE GOT TO GO TO THE BACK.

KLATTER

DIED
SKIN

CLICK.

MARDI
GRAS

11.

NGUUHHH. EEEYAAA... M.M.M.F.

FRANKLIN WAS COLD AS SNOW AND SWEATING LIKE A PIG. HE WANTED TO GET OUT OF THERE.

I....UHH, I...

YOU WANT A CAN OF WHUP-ASS, YOU SAY. WELL, FIRST YOU GOT TO SEE IT WORK. MAYBE THEN YOU DON'T WANT IT, BUT YOU GOT TO SEE!

"YOU REAL LUCKY, BOY, YOU KNOW THAT?!"

I....UHH, I...

YEAH, YOU REAL LUCKY. YOU SEE, I GOT TO USE ME A CAN OF WHUP-ASS THIS VERY NIGHT!

AND YOU GONNA GET TO WATCH IT WORK...FOR FREE!

THING IS, I DON'T USE WHUP-ASS MUCH. JUST THREE TIMES IN THE LAST FEW YEARS. ONLY THING THAT MAKES IT WORK IS *HATE*.

YOU KNOW HOW TO *HATE*, BOY?

I ASK YOU A QUESTION, BOY!

I, UH, I KNOW HOW TO HATE.

YEAH, I 'SPECT YOU KNOW HOW TO HATE, ALL RIGHT. I DON'T HATE MANY FOLKS, BUT YOU GOT TO HATE FOR THIS TO WORK. HATE'S A POWERFUL THING, AND I DON'T LIKE TO LET IT LOOSE!

IF YOU DON'T, UH, HATE, WHAT ABOUT, UH...

I DIDN'T HATE THAT HONKY HIT MY CAR. I JUST *SCARIN'* HIM...

...I COULDN'T OF USED THE WHUP-ASS ON HIM, WOULDN'T OF WORKED. BUT HE KNOWS ME, KNOWS WHAT I CAN DO. SO HE TOO SCARED TO TRY ANYTHING ON ME!

WHAT, UHH, ARE YOU?

I JUST A HOOLINGAN, THA'S ALL.

BUT THA'S *ENOUGH*.

13.

FRANKLIN DIDN'T HAVE ANY IDEA WHAT A *HOUNGAN* WAS, BUT HE WAS PRETTY SURE IT WASN'T ANYTHING HE WANTED TO KNOW ABOUT.

SO HE DIDN'T ASK.

CLATTER

CLATTER...

KNOCK!
KNOCK!

FRANKLIN HADN'T SEEN MANY WOMEN CLOSE-UP BEFORE, UNLESS YOU COUNTED HIS TEACHERS, AND THIS ONE DIDN'T LOOK AT ALL LIKE THEM. SHE LOOKED AS IF SHE COULD TEACH HIM A HELL OF A LOT, HOWEVER, AND JUST LOOKING AT HER GAVE HIM A *MONUMENTAL BONER!*

KLIK

WHO'S YOUR LITTLE FRIEND, EZRA?

YOU DON'T BE DOIN' THE ASKIN' HERE, WOMAN. I BE DOIN' THE ASKIN'.

WHAT YOU *ASKIN'*, EZRA?

WHAT BUSINESS OF YOURS *WHO I FUCK*, OLD MAN? I FUCK YOU ONCE A MONTH! YOU CAN'T GET IT UP MORE THAN THAT, NO MATTER HOW MUCH OF A *HOUNGAN* YOU ARE! AFTER THAT, I *FUCK* WHO I *PLEASE!!!*

I BE ASKIN' 'BOUT YOU *FUCKIN'* THAT SORRY-ASSED FRED COOGAN. 'BOUT YOU *FUCKIN'* THAT SHITASS TROY FARMER.

YOU WANNA TELL ME 'BOUT *THAT?!!*

SEE WHAT I MEAN, BOY?

14.

SCRAPE'. SCRITT...

YOU WOULDN'T USE THAT! YOU *WOULDN'T*!!!

AND DOORS LOCKED. AND I'D USE THIS CAN, SURE ENOUGH, 'CAUSE OF WHAT YOU DONE WITH *TROY FARMER* AND THAT GODDAM *FRED COOGAN*!

SHIK! SHAKE!

RATTLE RATTLE RATTLE...

YOU SAID IT JUST WORKED ON PEOPLE YOU HATE! YOU TOLD ME...

'POIT!

I HATE ANYBODY GO FUCKIN' AROUND ON *ME*!

YOU DON'T WANT TO DO THAT TO ME!

YES, I DO.

STOP IT! YOU *GOT* TO STOP IT!!!

CAN'T STOP IT. YOU CAN'T STOP HATE WHEN IT GETS A-LOOSE!

SNAP!!

NNÅAAAAAAHHH

YOU WANTED TO SEE *WHUP-ASS* AND NOW YOU SEEN IT.

THAT AIN'T NO WOMAN IN THE CAN, BOY. JUST HER SPIRIT. NOTHIN' LEFT OF HER BUT THAT. AND THAT OTHER SPIRIT, THE ONE I KEEP IN THE CAN...

...WELL, HE'S WHUPPIN' HER SPIRIT ASS FROM NOW TILL *DOOMSDAY!*

SPIT! SPAT!

SLURP!

HAND ME THAT CANDLE, BOY.

YIIII-II-I-I!

EEEEE-E-E-E!

ARRRGGHHH...

GARR-R-GG!

GONNA BE ONE HELL OF A RAW ASS BY THAT TIME, BOY, AND THAT'S WHAT A CAN OF *WHUP-ASS* DOES!

UH, HOW...UHH DOES IT WORK?

IT'S THE SPIRIT IN THE CAN, BOY. BUT YOU GOT TO DIRECT IT WITH *HATE*.

WHEN THAT SPIRIT COME OUT OF THE CAN, HE KNOWS WHO'S THE BOSS, AND WHOEVER YOU HATE THE MOST, *THAT'S* THE ONE HE GETS! SEE WHAT I MEAN, BOY?!!

LAST ONE I GOT LEFT, BOY. YOU BRING THE MONEY?

WELL, IT SURE AIN'T MUCH, BUT YOU LOOK LIKE A BOY NEEDS SOME WHUP-ASS. REMEMBER, YOU THINK ABOUT THE ONE YOU HATE THE MOST. THA'S THE ONE THE SPIRIT GOES FOR. *DON'T GET MIXED UP!*

I, UHH...I'LL REMEMBER.

17.

FRANKLIN HOPED THE LID WOULD HOLD WITHOUT WAX. EZRA HAD SAID IT WOULD BE GOOD FOR FOUR HOURS. WHICH WOULD BE FINE. FRANKLIN HAD A CANDLE AT HOME.

ALL RIGHT, FRA-A-A-NKLIN, THIS TIME I'M REALLY GOING TO KICK YOUR SCRAWNY ASS.

DO IT, BEN. KICK HIS SCRAWY LITTLE ASS!

FRANKLIN KNEW IT WAS GOING TO BE TOUGH DE-CIDING JUST WHO HE HATED THE MOST, BEN OR SHARLA. AND HE'D HAVE TO DECIDE QUICK!

UH, YOU AREN'T GOING TO, UHH, KICK, UH...ANYTHING! I'M GOING TO, UHH...OPEN UP A CAN OF W-WHUP-ASS AND PUT IT ON YOU!

POP!

WHAT THE HELL IS THAT?!!

SON OF A BITCH!!!

FRANKLIN STILL COULDN'T MAKE UP HIS MIND. HE KNEW HE HATED BEN, BUT HE ALSO HATED SHARLA. HE HATED THEM BOTH A LOT!

BUT AS FRANKLIN SUDDENLY REALIZED THE PERSON FRANKLIN HATED THE MOST WAS... HIMSELF! HE HATED HIS NAME, HE HATED HIS INABILITY TO MAKE UP HIS MIND, HE HATED HIS COWERDICE.

HE HATED THE FACT THAT HE WAS SO WEAK THAT HE COULDN'T EVEN HATE BEN AND SHARLA MORE THAN HE HATED...

SNAP!

HIMSELF!

19.

THE NEXT DAY A DUMP TRUCK DROPPED SEVERAL YARDS OF DIRT ON THE SCHOOL PARKING LOT. A GRADER SMOOTHED THE DIRT AND THAT AFTERNOON THEY BLACK-TOPPED THE LOT. NO ONE EVER SAW FRANKLIN AGAIN.

AND NO ONE MISSED HIM AT ALL.

20.

Chip Of Fools

A really swell guy and a wonderful writer, *Chet Williamson* is the writer of the novels *Reign*, *Dreamthorp*, and *Second Chance*. In comics he wrote *Aliens: Music of the Spears* (Dark Horse).

John Picacio is one of the talented newcomers in the world of self-published comics. His work has appeared in *Words & Pictures* (Maverick Studios) and *Book Of Dreams*. He is designing and illustrating the 30th anniversary edition of Michael Moorcock's *Behold The Man* for Mojo.

THOUGH THE DETECTIVES COULD READ SOME OF THE WORDS, THERE WERE OTHER THINGS THEY DIDN'T SEE.

THINGS THAT HAPPENED BEFORE THE WEB...

FROM: Ron
TO: ALL
Bastards screwed me again. THey sent my story back, and it was better than a lot of the ones they used in the first anthology. DOn´t know -when- I´ll get a break.

9:00

10:45

FROM: Carl
TO: Ron
Tough luck, Ron.

FROM: Edie
TO: ROn
FEel for YOu, Ron.

FROM: Mark
TO: Ron
Bummer, Ron. At least glad to see Julie got in.

FROM: Ron
TO: ALL
Glad about Julie? Yeah, and I guess Julies´ glad she was so -cozy- with Mr. Editor at the last Regicon. But don´t ask me -how- cozy. I´m just the village idiot.

THE NEXT NIGHT...

ACCESS DENIED

THOUGH HE DOESN'T KNOW WHY, OTHERS DO.

FROM: Mark
TO: Edie
Where's Ron? Thought he'd be bitching and moaning again tonight.

FROM: Edie
TO: Mark
THe sysop locked him out. It's not bad enough he was bringing everybody down. but he was getting libelous too. Why? YOu miss hhim?

FROM: Mark
TO: Edie
No.

IT WAS THE THIRD BOARD RON HAD BEEN SHUT OUT OF.

AND IT WASN'T WORTH THE ACCESS CHARGES...

...IF THERE WAS NOBODY TO CARE.

THE LOCAL BOARDS HAD NO CHAT MODES.

OU COULD PAGE THE SYSOP.

[C]hat with SysOp
[>
[P]lease wait while paging SysOp..]
...SysOp Not Available. Try again later.

BUT THEY WERE SELDOM THERE.

IF EVER.

...finally got it into a gallery, it just -sat- there.
...same thing happened with my last few rugs...
...nobody appreciates anything -different-. My novel's been to a dozen publishers...
I know how you must feel.
I know how hard all of you work.
And then to be so unappreciated... it must be very hard.
But at least you know there's someone who understands
and who believes in you
RON FELT AT HOME ON THE WEB. THE OTHERS WERE SO LIKE HIM.
AND CHARLOTTE HELD THEM TOGETHER,
SYMPATHIZED WITH THEM, PRAISED THEM...
...LOVED THEM.

SOON RON WAS SPENDING ALL OF HIS FREE TIME ON THE BOARD.

LAST ON: 3-12-95
TOTAL #: 46
ATTEMPT: 1
START: 23:05:14
CURRENT: 23:05:17

AND NO MATTER WHEN HE WENT ON...

...CHARLOTTE WAS ALWAYS THERE.

HE STOPPED WRITING COMPLETELY.

AND READING.

FOR IT WAS MORE FULFILLING...

...TO TELL CHARLOTTE ABOUT WHAT HE HAD WRITTEN...

...AND THE GLORIOUS THINGS HE *WOULD* WRITE.

SOMEDAY.

YEH... YEH... NO SHIT...

TWO OTHERS. SAME M.O. -- MODEM LINES OPEN, RAGBAGS LIKE THIS ON THE FLOOR.

GET THEIR NAMES?

PAUL WARREN AND LINDA CAPRIOTTI.

I SUGGEST WE HAUL ASSES OVER TO CHARLOTTE'S. LET'S GET THE ADDRESS FROM THE TRACE, AND CALL IN FOR A WARRANT.

THE PHONE NUMBER IS THAT OF A RICHARD SEARS.

THE ADDRESS IS 427 BEECHWOOD.

MR. SEARS?

YES?

DAMN.

WHAT IS IT?

LOCKED UP ON ME.

HIT CONTROL-ALT-DELETE.

NOTHING.

IT DOES THIS SOMETIMES. JUST POWER IT DOWN AND WAIT FOR A MINUTE. THEN RESTART IT.

THEY TURN THE MACHINE OFF. AND THE SOUND OF THE FAN STOPS.

AND IN THE SUDDEN SILENCE...

THERE COMES A SOFT, SKITTERING SOUND.

WHAT THE HELL IS *THAT?*

IT'S INSIDE THE CPU.

I'LL OPEN THE CASE.

THE SCREWS COME OUT...

... AND THE COVER SLIDES OFF.

JESUS.

THEY LOOK LIKE...

Man With Legs

The writer of many novels, *Al Sarrantonio* lives in New York State. His short stories have appeared in *Heavy Metal, Whispers, Razored Saddles, Shadows, Year's Best Horror Stories* and others.

Doug Potter is either very obscure or somewhat famous depending upon who you talk to. Doug was the writer and artist of *Chips-N-Vanilla* (Kitchen Sink), *Denizens Of Deep City* (Kitchen Sink), and *Messozoic* (Kitchen Sink). He has also done work for Marvel and Dark Horse.

THE MAN WITH LEGS

script by Al Sarrantonio   drawing by Doug Potter

I SAW HIM WHEN WE WENT BY IN THE SCHOOL BUS THIS AFTERNOON. HE WAS STANDING ON THE PORCH OF THE HOUSE, AND HE LOOKED AT ME AS THE BUS WENT BY.

I DON'T BELIEVE YOU.

YOU'LL SEE...

I STILL SAY YOU'RE WRONG.

SIT.

IT'S BEAUTIFUL.

There were snow valleys and peaks, and stiff, hard drifts of white that sloped up the sides of buildings and stayed there.

BRRRR!

BEAUTIFUL...

There were upside-down icecream cone icicles that hung frozen from corners, dipping to just touch the drifts below.

All the world was a snowball, an ice shell six inches deep made of snowmen and newspaper delivery boys in parkas and ski boots.

SIT DOWN.

WE HAVE TO GET BACK TO THE BUS SOON...

SHE TOLD US YOU DIED.

THAT'S INTERESTING...

SHE SAID THE TRAIN YOU WERE ON HIT THE BACK OF ANOTHER TRAIN.

WE HEARD YOUR LEGS HAD BEEN CUT OFF!

WERE YOU HURT IN A TRAIN WRECK?

IS THAT WHY YOU LIMP?

NO...

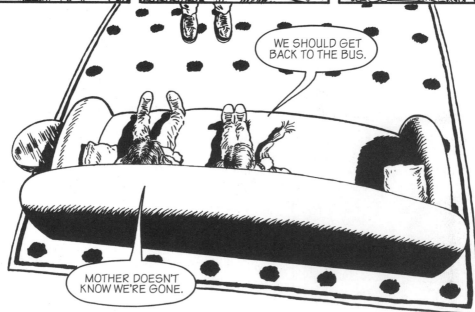

Willie moved slowly, fingering the walls...

...until a sound down one corridor pulled him toward it...

...a high, singing sound and, behind that, the sound of metal against metal.

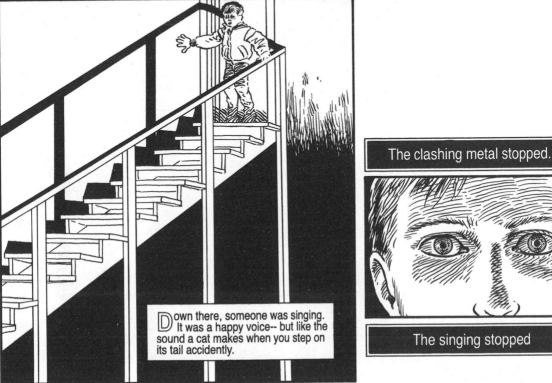

Down there, someone was singing. It was a happy voice-- but like the sound a cat makes when you step on its tail accidently.

The clashing metal stopped.

The singing stopped

There was a grunt and the sound of something being lashed and tied, the whipping of ropes, and then footsteps.

Little, dancing footsteps, more grunting, and then steadier steps.

Someone was on the stairs.

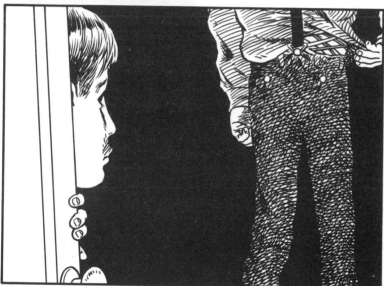

Willie counted to fifty and then emerged from the shadows.

There were no sounds in the cellar.

OH, NO...

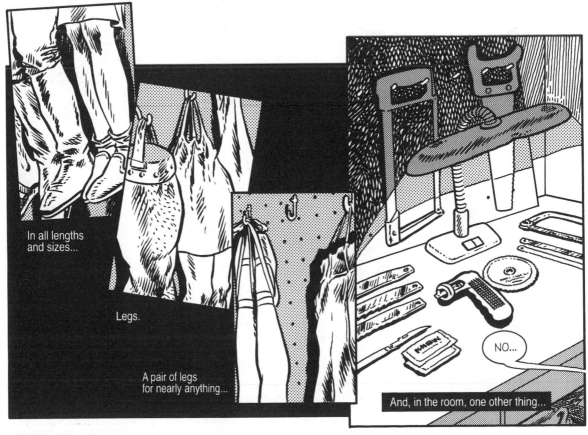

From above, a sound sounded.

NELLIE !

SHHH !

NELLIE, HE--

I KNOW. HE TOLD ME EVERYTHING. HE WANTS US TO STAY. HE'S NOT BAD, WILLIE.

MOST OF HIS LEGS HE DUG UP, OR FOUND ON DEAD PEOPLE. IF WE STAY, HE'LL BE FATHER MOST OF THE TIME. I NEED THAT, WILLIE.

NO !

I NEED HIM TO BE FATHER, WILLIE.

I WANT TO GO HOME !

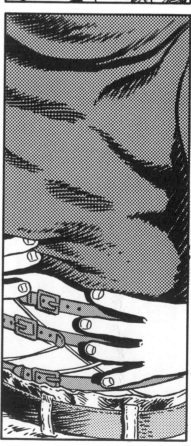

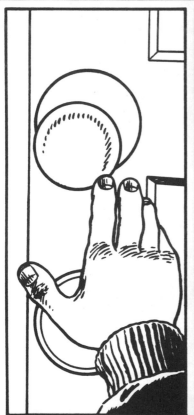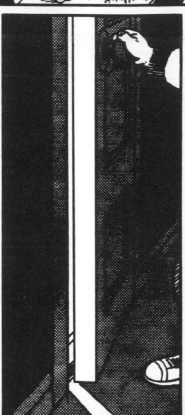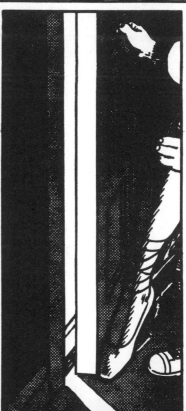

WALK WITH ME, WON'T YOU?

King Of The Cows

A former Campbell nominee, *Scott Cupp* is one of the best weird short fiction writers in the country. His stories include the now classic "Thirteen Days Of Glory," which almost got his Texas citizenship revoked, and "Jimmy and Me and The Nigger Man," a cross between Lovecraft, Huckleberry Finn, Frankenstein, the Tar Baby, and Disney's *Fantasia*.

A perfect match for Scott Cupp, with his subdued weirdness, *Matthew Guest* wrote and illustrated the strange *Suburban Voodoo Tales* (Fantagraphics) and has done work for *Duplex Planet* (Fantagraphics).

I stayed busy with the stock trying to meet the demand for the holiday.

Good hard work is its own reward.

One more bull was all we needed to finish out the work for the day.

The cattle seemed restless, milling around aimlessly, almost as if there were a storm on the horizon.

THUD

BOBBY!

I'M SORRY!

ARE YOU HURT?

Phil had some question about an order which we resolved.

My head throbbed but no major damage appeared to have been done.

SLAUGHTER HIM!

WELL, DIE, IF YOU MUST!

I WILL NOT STOP THIS FROM HAPPENING!

THUD!

I worked in a BLIND RAGE...

I SLASHED his throat and WATCHED HIS LIFE DRAIN AWAY...

into a vat of CRIMSON FLUID.

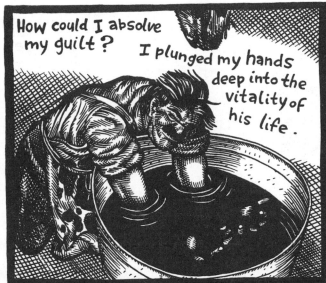

 I had to get home and make sure Peggy was SAFE.

We made our way upstairs...

We prayed for the remainder of that day.

Soon, the heavens opened and God unleashed his wrath on our small town.

We heard tales of those who saw ghastly visions of the dead cows who walked through the storm.

I bear the mark of his death on my hands.

It is Saturday now. Tomorrow is Sunday... Easter Sunday. I must be up at the dawn and go to the slaughterhouse.

I AM AFRAID OF WHAT I WILL NOT FIND.

In Repose

By trade a pyro-technician and freelance journalist, *Marc Paoletti's* first fiction story appeared in *Young Blood.* He is currently the editor of *System Shock* (Tuscany).

Michael Lark got his start at Caliber doing his critically acclaimed series *Airwaves,* and has become one of the most demanded artists in the country. His recent work includes *Shade, The Changing Man* (DC/Vertigo) and *Little Sister* (Byron Preiss). Upcoming projects include art in *Occurrences* (Mojo) and a new ongoing series for DC/Vertigo.

IN REPOSE

written by
MARC PAOLETTI

illustrated & lettered by
MICHAEL LARK

London, 1880.

Table.

Goddamn birds! I'll bet they shit all over every-thing!

Name?

Toastie's name is Emma Crane. She ran into a burnin' house after her cat....

...Funny thing was the cat was already out.

Silly cunt. She deserved it, then.

Go.

It is delightful to make your acquaintance.

My name is Horace Dusk. You may call me Horace.

I will be reconstructing your face, and I must confess that you are fortunate to have found me.

You are quite a handsome woman, Emma, if I may be so bold.

Yes, there are countless morticians in London, but only I will be able to restore you.

Because, you see...

...it is only I who understands the true essence of beauty.

Do you have a family? A woman so beautiful is bound to have a husband.

Myself? No, but thank you for asking. I have been courting my beloved Alice for almost two years now.

She is everything I could ever want in a woman.

It was love at first sight. I know that sounds horribly trite, but it was, oh yes. The minute I saw her--

chirp?

Ah, there.

What do you think?

Later that evening.

Beautiful...

For you, a long-stemmed dozen, warm and red.

A music-sewn daffodil, singing blossoms--

Agh!

Oh!

Who--

The birds!

Excuse me?

Please stay.

It's all right, really. You just took me by surprise.

You mentioned the birds. They're so beautiful, especially when they sing.

Sometimes I lie here and watch them for hours.

They seem so happy up there, so free.

I have a few.

How wonderful!

Horace Dusk.

How rude of me! My name is Laura Fetter. It is a pleasure to meet you, Mr. Dusk.

Fetter?

I'm Dr. William Fetter's daughter.

Yes, *the* Dr. Fetter. I hope that doesn't make you uncomfortable.

No.

Good.

Laura.

Acrocephalus Shoenoboenus.

The warbler? How sweet!

I have a wonderful idea! Would you be my escort to my father's dinner party this evening? It's one of his political gatherings.

Those people are so boring, and you wouldn't believe how dense. Do come, Mr. Dusk.

Horace.

Please, Horace. It would be so much more fun if you were there.

If you insist, dear Laura.

That evening.

There you are, Horace!

I want to introduce you to my father.

Dad, this is Horace Dusk. The gentleman I met in the park.

Horace, this is my father, Dr. William Fetter.

A pleasure to meet you, Mr. Dusk. I am familiar with your work.

This is Sir Thomas Flitcroft of the Ministry of Trade, Sir Charles Osborne of the Ministry of War, and his wife.

You're not a radical I hope, Mr. Dusk. What they're inciting in the laborers is an abomination!

A cow and three acres my ass!

It's socialism, pure and simple. That and the trade deficit--

Mr. Dusk is a mortician.

His reputation in this area is sound.

STOP!

Of course it will not eat, you simpleton!

The bird's indigenous surroundings are lush and foresty, it's main source of sustenance fruit and insects!

Lorries live only in mated pairs deep within the hollow of a fruit tree.

You cannot expect a bird so specialized to live in tropical conditions to adapt to your pathetically inadequate surroundings.

It languishes because you are suffocating it, you oaf!

What if you were taken from your precious manse and trapped in the Sahara Desert?

This outburst is most--

I know what you are trying to do, Dr. Fetter.

Oh yes. The Lory's plumage is breathtaking.

But how sophomoric to try to contain that which cannot be contained. How truly sad!

By caging the bird, you have taken away its habits, struggles, joys, freedoms--

--those very things that make it beautiful!

To appreciate the Lory, to appreciate anything-- to truly covet beauty-- you must capture its essence and let the body go.

Its freedom is only an illusion, however, for you will have gained something far more impressive than the physical.

You will have captured its soul, and from that point forward, that creature will be in thrall to you.

Otherwise, the image you see is but a shadow of true existence.

I think he just quoted Tennyson.

Really?

Yes. Well. I believe dinner is being served in the dining room. So if you'll all move...

...apologize...

No one has ever stood up to my father that way. You were wonderful!

Would you mind showing me your home?

I--

Your birds. I would so like to see them.

A short time later.

Oh Horace, they're beautiful!

Yes.

To the essence of beauty.

Of course, Laura. I would be happy to read to you.

"She blinks, and we see sudden flowers

"Watercolor running rainbows To a melody of sun as wind whips grass

"Singing blossom blues There is only her."

·END·

Trolling

F. Paul Wilson is the author of several highly acclaimed novels, including *The Keep*. Among his other books are *The Touch, Black Wind*, and most recently *The Select*.

The talented *Bill D. Fountain's* work first appeared in *Creature Features* (Mojo) which was soon followed by *The Sound Of Coming Darkness* (Blackbird), his sequel to Edgar Allan Poe's *The Cask Of Amontillado*. Bill's next project is the art for a selection of Poe's work in *The Tell-tale Heart & Other Works* (Mojo).

TROLLING

STORY BY F. PAUL WILSON
IMAGES BY BILL D. FOUNTAIN

THE CARLY NOT LIKE NEEDLE MANS. SMELL BAD. MAKE MESSES.

GET LOST FOOL!

TOLD YOU.... ONLY ENOUGH HERE FOR ONE!

NOT HAVE PRETTY FACES.

OUTTA HERE!!

'SAMATTA? YOU DEAF OR....

OH GOD, NO!!

CAN I PLEASE, RICKY? CAN I?

LOOOOCEEE, I TOL' YOU A THOUSAN' TIMES, ABSOLUTELY NOT!

BACK SO SOON, CARLY?

YESH, JESHI. HOW COME YOU KNOW TO LAUGH?

WAAAAH RICKY!

MY DEAR GIRL, I SAW THESE SO MANY TIMES WHEN I HAD MY SIGHT, THAT I CAN REPLAY EVERY SCENE IN MY HEAD.

FLIK!

SOMETIMES I HARDLY MISS MY SIGHT AT ALL. AND THERE ARE TIMES WHEN BLINDNESS CAN EVEN BE...

...A BLESSING.

LETSH GO.

AGAIN? WE WENT TROLLING LAST WEEK, CARLY. ARE WE OUT OF MONEY ALREADY?

YESH.

AND NOW THE LATEST ON THE FACELIFT KILLER...

PRETTY FACE. THE CARLY LIKE HER FACE. THE CARLY WANT HER FACE.

NO SMOKING IN HERE SWEETIE.

UP YOURS.

SOMEDAY THE CARLY HAVE FACE LIKE HER.

WHAT A RUDE YOUNG WOMAN. I'M GLAD YOU'RE A NICE GIRL, CARLY...

FACELIFT KIL
WHEN WILL HE STR

HEY, LADY. YOU REALLY BLIND?

WHO'S THAT? DO I KNOW YOU?

NO YOU DON'T KNOW ME. BUT LEMME ASK YOU: AREN'T YOU 'FRAID SOMEBODY'S GONNA—

...STEAL YOUR POCKETBOOK?

HEY!!!

LET GO OF THAT! THAT'S MINE!!

HEY YO, JOEY. DIS BITCH IS STRONG! HOW 'BOUT A LIL' HELP HERE, MAN?

JOEY?

WHERE THE FU—

GAAAAAAK!

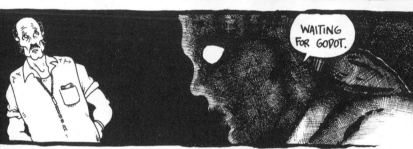

WHO'S THAT? DO I KNOW YOU?

SAY, IT'S AROUND THE BEGINNIN' OF THE MONTH, AIN'T IT?

YOU SHOULDA GOT YOUR SOCIAL SECURITY CHECK BY NOW. LET'S SEE HOW MUCH THEY GAVE YOU.

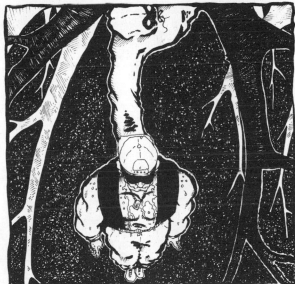

ALL DONE JESHI...

Green Brother

A truly unique writer and personage, *Howard Waldrop* has a large and loyal cult following. He's sort of like Cyril Kornbluth meets Philip Jose Farmer, but different. In short there is no one quite like Howard. His work includes two novels (*Texas-Israeli War: 1999* with Jake Saunders and *Them Bones*) and a ton of short stories which have been collected in *Howard Who?*, *All About Strange Monsters In The Recent Past*, and *Night Of The Cooters*.

Another odd Texas duck, *Steve Utley* was one of the most important young SF writers in the early 1970's until he all but stopped writing in 1980. In recent years Utley has started to write and sell his stories again. And there was much rejoicing.

One of the best "pure" pencillers in comics, *John Lucas'* first works include several stories and covers for the Absolute Comics titles. He then did a comic he'd rather not talk about. Future works include stories in *The Wild West Show* (Mojo), *Occurrences* (Mojo), *Big Justice* (Adhesive), and the cover to *JAB* Number 6 (Adhesive).

1907

MY *GREAT-GRANDFATHER* SELDOM BLANKET, TELLS THIS STORY OF THE *OLD* DAYS.

I AM TALKING *NOW* OF THE TIME THE PEOPLE WERE FIGHTING THE *SOLDIERS*...

FIGHTING ABOUT THE *ROAD* AND THE *FORT* THE SOLDIERS PUT THROUGH OUR *HUNTING* LANDS.

IN THOSE DAYS, I WAS A BIG *MEDICINE* CHIEF OF MY PEOPLE.

IN THOSE DAYS, *MAGIC* STILL WORKED FOR US.

GRAND-FATHER!

YES? SOMETHING EXCITES YOU?

Green Brother
ADAPTED FROM HOWARD WALDROP'S STORY BY
STEVEN UTLEY - WRITER
JOHN LUCAS - PENCILS AND INKS
BRAD THOMTE - LETTERS

ONION BOY... IS NO LONGER ONION BOY! HE WENT OFF... AND CAME BACK, AND NOW... NOW HE IS FALCON FOOT.

I SHALL TRY TO REMEMBER HIS NEW NAME. IS HE CHANGED MUCH?

NO, EXCEPT NOW HE HAS A MEDICINE BUNDLE WITH A FALCON FOOT IN IT.

HE SAID THE HAWK MUST HAVE BEEN SHOT, BECAUSE AS IT FLEW OVER, IT'S FOOT FELL TO THE GROUND BEFORE HIM.

A GOOD SIGN. DID HE DREAM OF FLYING? USUALLY, PEOPLE WHO TAKE BIRD NAMES HAVE VISIONS OF FLYING WHILE ON THEIR QUEST.

I FORGOT TO ASK HIM.

NOT IMPORTANT.

GRANDFATHER, WHAT WAS YOUR VISION QUEST LIKE?

OH, THAT WAS A LONG TIME AGO. I SAW A MAN THAT DID NOT NEED A BLANKET IN THE WINTER.

THEY'RE COMING OUT NOW.

BUT NOT TO *FIGHT*...YOU'LL SEE.

HEY-A!

HEY-A!

YAH! YAH! YAH!

WOMEN SHOOT BETTER THAN THAT!

COWARDS! COME AND FIGHT!

GRANDSON, WHAT IS IT?

I DON'T *KNOW*...I...

IS THE *EXCITEMENT* TOO MUCH FOR YOU?

NO, GRANDFATHER... I...I DIDN'T PAY MUCH ATTENTION...

GRANDSON, COME AND *EAT*.

NO, I HAVE SEEN A FLYCATCHER CATCH A WINGED INSECT. TODAY, I THINK, *WE* MAY CATCH SOME SOLDIERS.

PAW!

SEND OUT **MORE** SOLDIERS TOMORROW SO WE CAN KILL **THEM**, TOO!

WHY, HELLO, GRANDSON, YOU MISSED A GOOD FIGHT THREE MORNINGS AGO.

GRANDFATHER...

YES.

COULD YOU HELP ME WITH MY **NEW** NAME?

MOST PEOPLE DO NOT **NEED** HELP WITH THEIRS.

THAT IS BECAUSE THEY HAVE SEEN A SPIRIT ANIMAL AND **KNOW** ITS NAME. I SAW AN ANIMAL, BUT I DO NOT KNOW ITS NAME.

THAT **IS** A PROBLEM. PERHAPS I CAN HELP.

CAN I **SLEEP** NOW?

SLEEP.

I WILL TELL YOU ABOUT THE ANIMAL **LATER**.

THIS PLACE IS GOING TO SMELL **BAD** ALL SUMMER.

I ROAMED THE HILLS... CHANTED... DID **NOT** SLEEP.

I PUT SHARP ROCKS BETWEEN MY TOES AND SCOURED MY EYES WITH BRAMBLES TO KEEP MYSELF **AWAKE**.

"BUT ONE DID NOT COME FOR A LONG TIME."

I LAY OVER A ROCK WITH MY HEAD DOWN TO GET A *VISION*,...

I HEARD *VOICES*, BUT IT WAS ALWAYS THE *WIND* WHEN I LISTENED CLOSER.

THEN I *TURNED*, GRANDFATHER... IN THE DIRECTION OF THE BIG DIRT ROAD.

"AND I SAW IT."

WHERE IS FALL COLT GOING?

HIS NAME IS NOT FALL COLT ANY MORE.

WHAT IS IT THEN?

HE IS GOING TO FIND THAT OUT.

PAW

HE HAS BEEN ON HIS VISION QUEST, BUT IT WAS INCONCLUSIVE.

HE IS TROUBLED.

HAS HE LOST HIS *WITS*?

GREAT MYSTERY PROBLEMS.

Oh.

I AM GOING DOWN THERE TO SEE IF HE IS ALL RIGHT.

BETTER TAKE HIM SOME FOOD AND HIS *BOW*. THE SOLDIERS MIGHT SEND SOME- ONE OUT TO *HURT* HIM.

THEY ARE PROBABLY AFRAID HE IS GOING TO *BURROW* UP INSIDE THEIR FORT AND KILL THEM IN THEIR SLEEP.

HOW IS YOUR SON?

HE IS *STILL* DIGGING.

I DID NOT KNOW ONE PERSON COULD MOVE SO MUCH DIRT.

I KEPT MY EYES TURNED AWAY WHEN I SAW WHAT HE WAS DOING. THERE ARE PARTS OF STORM BEASTS AROUND THERE. HE IS DIGGING *AMONG* THEM.

STORM BEASTS! THAT *IS* BAD. THERE WAS NO THUNDER OR LIGHTNING IN HIS STORY.

DO YOU THINK THE *GREAT MYSTERY* HAS DRIVEN MY SON MAD?

I DO NOT THINK THE *GREAT MYSTERY* IS PUNISH- ING YOUR SON, BUT THERE IS *MAGIC* AT WORK THERE, AND IT'S SO *GREAT*, I'D RATHER NOT BE AROUND WHEN IT HAPPENS.

BUT YOU WILL.

OF COURSE I WILL.

GRANDFATHER.

I NEED SOME GREAT MEDICINE WORKED.

A STORM IS COMING AND YOU ARE WORKING AMONG THE **STORM-BEASTS**. YOU ARE GOING TO NEED MORE POWER THAN *I* CAN ASK FOR.

BUT I WILL SEE WHAT I CAN DO. HAVE YOU THOUGHT OF A NEW *NAME* YET?

I AM GOING TO BE CALLED GREEN BROTHER.

GREEN BROTHER IS A *GOOD* NAME.

GUIDE ME, GRANDSON-- I AM GOING TO *CLOSE* MY EYES. IF I SEE THE SPIRIT ANIMAL ALL AT *ONCE*, IT WILL BE *EASIER* ON ME.

I WILL EITHER *LIVE* OR *DIE* IN THAT INSTANT.

IT IS *BEFORE* YOU, GRANDFATHER.

IS IT *TERRIBLE?*

NOT ONCE YOU GET *USED* TO IT.

MAKE *MAGIC* WITH IT.

WHAT DO YOU WISH IT TO *DO?*

I WANT IT TO *WALK* UP THIS RAMP AND *ACROSS* THE ROAD AND INTO THE *FORT.*

THAT WILL PROBABLY *IMPRESS* THE SOLDIERS.

NOW STAND *BACK.* THIS IS GOING TO BE *TOUGH.*

AND I NEED *LOTS* OF ROOM.

GREAT MYSTERY, IT IS *I*, YOUR SON. I AM *SMALL* BEFORE THE STORM, AS ARE *ALL* MEN AND WOMEN. REMEMBER THE THINGS THE PEOPLE HAVE DONE IN *GRATITUDE* FOR YOUR BLESSINGS.

I THANK YOU FOR THE *MANY* TIMES YOU HAVE WRESTLED *DEATH* FOR ME. I ASK YOU *NOW* TO REMEMBER THE THINGS THE SOLDIERS HAVE DONE TO US.

YEARS AGO, WE HAD A BIG MEETING WITH THE *WHITE MEN*, AND TOUCHED THE *PEN*, AND HAD A BIG SUPPER, AND THEY BROUGHT US BLANKETS AND HARDTACK AND BEANS.

THEN THEY BUILT THE *ROAD* THROUGH OUR BEST HUNTING LANDS. THE ROAD FILLED WITH WAGONS AND *WHITE* PEOPLE WHO LET US KNOW THEY DIDN'T LIKE US. THE ROAD MADE THE *BUFFALO* SKITTISH TOO.

THE SOLDIERS CAME OUT WHILE WE WERE IN OUR *WINTER* HUNTING GROUNDS AND BUILT THEIR *FORT*. WE ASKED THEM IF THEY WERE GOING TO *MOVE* BEFORE IT GOT COLD AGAIN.

THEY SAID WE HAD *AGREED* TO THE BUILDING OF THE FORT AND THE ROAD, BUT NONE OF US REMEMBERS THE SUBJECT *EVER* COMING UP.

WE HAVE *SHOWN* THE SOLDIERS HOW *ANNOYED* WE ARE BY HAVING A *WAR* WITH THEM.

NOW I AM ASKING *YOU* TO INTERCEDE THROUGH THE STORM BEAST BEFORE ME.

"SOON AFTER, THE SOLDIERS LEFT THE FORT, AND WE WENT AND BURNED IT TO THE GROUND."

THE NEXT SPRING, WE SIGNED *ANOTHER* TREATY WITH THE WHITE MEN, BUT OF COURSE *THAT* JUST LED TO MORE FIGHTING LATER.

THIS CREATURE YOU DESCRIBE, THE *STORM BEAST,* SOUNDS LIKE WHAT SCIENTISTS-- *WISE WHITE MEN*-- CALL A DINOSAUR.

LIKE THAT LIZARD OVER THERE, BUT MUCH *BIGGER* AND *FIERCER.*

MY GREAT-GRANDFATHER SAYS HE IS *IGNORANT* OF MANY WHITE MAN'S THINGS, BUT AS LONG AS THERE IS A *BLUE SKY* ABOVE, AS LONG AS THE GREAT MYSTERY *SMILES,*...

HE KNOWS THE THING HE SAW IN THE PIT WAS *NO* LIZARD.

OF COURSE NOT.

IN *THOSE* DAYS, MAGIC STILL WORKED FOR US.

HE SAYS TO GO BOTHER SOMEONE *ELSE* NOW. HE WANTS ME TO TURN HIM TOWARDS THE SUN, SO HE CAN *SMOKE.*

And I Only Am Escaped To Tell Thee

One of the most important and prestigious science fiction and fantasy writers, *Roger Zelazny's* career ranges over 40 years. He has won both the Hugo and Nebula and is the creator of *Amber.* It would be impossible to list all Roger's stories but recent works include *Wilderness* (with Gerald Hausmann), *Night Of The Lonesome October,* and a forthcoming *Amber* comic book series.

By day a lawyer for the State of Texas, *Paul O. Miles* is secretly a very talented writer. This is his first professional work. He'd prefer that the whole world didn't know he wrote a comic book story.

Barb & Theodore Spoon are the famed husband and wife art team noted for their work on several small press erotic comics. Current projects include the design of the first sex shop in Moscow to feature genital piercing.

And I Am Only Escaped To Tell Thee

Based on a short story
by Roger Zelazny

SCRIPT BY PAUL O. MILES
ART BY BARBE & THEODORE SPOON
LETTERS BY BRAD THOMTE

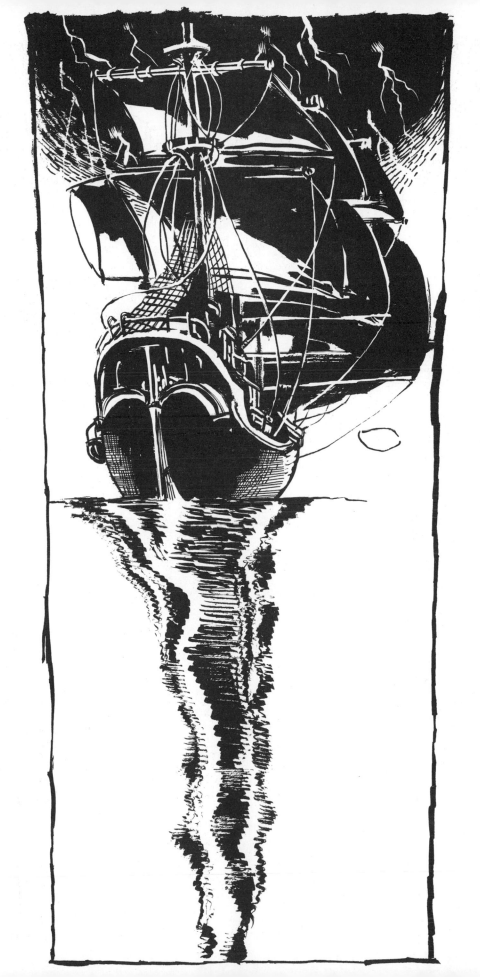

Case Of The Dancing Corpse

Jerry Prosser's writing career began with the publication of the controversial *Exquisite Corpse* (Dark Horse). Since then Jerry has written a wide variety of things ranging from *Aliens* to *X*. Currently, he is the writer of *Animal Man* (DC/Vertigo).

Recently re-locating to the San Fransisco Bay area, *Jason Morgan* has done illustrations for various British magazines. This is his first published comic book story.

THE CASE OF THE DANCING CORPSE

IT WAS LATE ON A JULY NIGHT IN 1940. THE NIGHT THAT CHANGED MY LIFE.

I WAS WALKING MY BEAT IN HARLEM, WHEN A DETECTIVE NAMED DOYLE CAME UP TO ME. I RECOGNIZED HIM FROM THE PRECINCT, BUT I DIDN'T KNOW HIM VERY WELL. KEPT TO HIMSELF. DOYLE SAID HE NEEDED ME TO COME WITH HIM. SOMETHING IMPORTANT, HE SAID.

DOYLE BROUGHT ME TO THE OLD PLACE ON LEXINGTON, NEAR MOUNT HARRIS PARK. THERE WERE PLENTY OF STORIES ABOUT IT IN THE NEIGHBORHOOD, BUT NOBODY I KNEW HAD EVER BEEN INSIDE, OR EVEN KNEW WHO LIVED THERE.

I WAS ABOUT TO FIND OUT.

DOYLE SEEMED A LITTLE NERVOUS, LIKE HE WAS AFRAID OF GOING IN. I WAS EXCITED.

WHAT'S YOUR FIRST NAME, OFFICER CLARKE?

JOHN, SIR.

ENOUGH WITH THAT "SIR" STUFF, JOHN. JUST CALL ME BILL.

WHAT ARE WE DOING HERE ...BILL?

YOU'LL FIND OUT SOON ENOUGH.

JUST KEEP YOUR EYES OPEN...

AND YOUR MOUTH SHUT.

GOOD EVENING, DETECTIVE DOYLE. DOCTOR D. IS EXPECTING YOU.

STORY BY JERRY PROSSER   ART BY JASON MORGAN   LETTERING BY DOUG POTTER

WHEN I COULD FINALLY OPEN MY EYES, THEY HURT.

THERE WAS SOMETHING STRANGE ABOUT THE LIGHT. IT WAS EVERYWHERE, BUT I COULDN'T TELL WHERE IT WAS COMING FROM.

I DIDN'T KNOW WHERE I WAS, BUT IT SEEMED FAMILIAR SOMEHOW.

LIKE I'D BEEN THERE BEFORE.

I COULDN'T TELL HOW LONG I HAD BEEN WAITING. MINUTES? HOURS? I HAD NO SENSE OF TIME. EVENTUALLY ONE OF THE DOORS OPENED, AND **HE** ENTERED THE ROOM.

HELLO, OFFICER CLARKE. I'M SORRY TO HAVE KEPT YOU.

HIS VOICE WAS DIFFERENT NOW. STRONG, CONFIDENT. HE GAVE THE IMPRESSION OF ENERGY AND VITALITY.

WHERE AM I? WHERE'S DOYLE? WHAT ARE YOU DOING?

CALM YOURSELF, OFFICER CLARKE. WE ARE IN A ROOM IN YOUR MIND. ONE IN WHICH YOU SPEND MOST OF YOUR TIME. A BIT SQUALID, I MUST SAY. WE ARE GOING ON A LITTLE TRIP, YOU AND I.

TRIP? WHAT ARE YOU TALK ABOUT?

THIS PLACE IS IN QUITE A STATE. YOU REALLY HAVE QUITE A CLUTTERED CONSCIOUSNESS, OFFICER CLARKE.

IF YOU LIKE, I'LL HELP YOU TIDY IT UP WHEN WE RETURN. MAYBE VISIT SOME OF THE OTHER ROOMS...

NOW, JUST RELAX. PLEASE, DO NO RESIST ME. IF YOU DO, YOU WILL D.

I DIDN'T WANT TO, BUT I CLOSED MY EYES. WHEN I OPENED THEM...

WAS BY THE HUDSON RIVER, I COULD SMELL IT, BUT DIDN'T SEEM LIKE I WAS SMELLING WITH MY OWN OSE. I LOOKED AT MY HANDS, BUT THEY DIDN'T FEEL IGHT; LIKE THEY WEREN'T MINE ANYMORE.

IT WAS WHEN I TOOK A STEP CLOSER TO THE WAREHOUSE THAT I REALIZED I WASN'T IN CONTROL OF MY OWN BODY.

HE WAS. THEN I HEARD HIM TALKING TO ME FROM SOMEWHERE INSIDE MY HEAD.

IT WILL TAKE SOME GETTING USED TO. BUT I ASSURE YOU, I WON'T HARM YOUR BODY.

WE GOT INTO THE BUILDING WITH NO PROBLEMS. A GUARD EVEN LED US TO THE STAIRS. NOW I UNDERSTOOD WHY HE WANTED MY BODY. AS A POLICEMAN, HE COULD GET BACK TO THE CRIME SCENE UNDISTURBED.

HE KEPT TALKING TO ME. HIS VOICE WAS REASSURING.

YOU SHOULD BE ABLE TO SEE, BUT DO NOT FIGHT ME FOR CONTROL. JUST RELAX. LIKE A PASSENGER IN A CAR, ENJOY THE RIDE.

THE ROOM SMELLED AWFUL. THE HEAT HAD REALLY RIPENED IT UP. THERE WERE FLIES EVERYWHERE. I WAS ALMOST GLAD MY NOSE BELONGED TO A STRANGER.

E WAS TALKING. I COULDN'T TELL IF IT WAS TO ME OR TO HIMSELF.

WHAT WERE YOU UP TO **HERR MANN**?

SOMETHING OUT OF YOUR LEAGUE, I'LL WAGER.

WERE YOU EVER IN TIBET, HERR MANN?

DAMN GERMANS... SHOULD STICK WITH THEIR **SEX MAGICK**.

OFFICER CLARKE, I'LL NEED TO SEE THE OTHER BODY. CAN YOU DIRECT US TO THE MORGUE?

I WOKE UP IN ANOTHER UNFAMILIAR ROOM.

BUT THIS TIME I HAD A PRETTY GOOD IDEA WHERE I WAS.

ESPECIALLY SINCE I DIDN'T FEEL *HIM* IN MY HEAD ANYMORE AND MY BODY ONCE AGAIN BELONGED TO ME.

YOU LOOK BETTER.

WHAT HAPPENED? HOW DID YOU CONTROL MY BODY? HOW DID I GET BACK HERE?

ANCIENT TIBETAN RITE. THE **ROLANG.** THE CORPSE WHO STANDS UP... DANCES. TONGUE FROM CORPSE DRIED. POWERFUL WEAPON FOR SORCERER.

GERMAN TRIED THE RITE. NOT STRONG ENOUGH. SHOULD NOT HAVE LOCKED HIMSELF IN WITH CORPSE. BAD BUSINESS. STUPID.

STRANGE THINGS HAPPENING IN GERMANY.

WHAT DID HE DO IT FOR? WHY DID YOU *WE* DO IT?

ALWAYS BE CAREFUL WHAT YOU SAY. NO MORE POWERFUL WEAPON...

THAN HUMAN TONGUE.

THAT WAS THE END OF MY FIRST MEETING WITH DOCTOR D.

THERE HAVE BEEN OTHER MEETINGS. SOME I HAVE PERMISSION TO RELATE. OTHERS WILL COST ME **MY** TONGUE.

Heilage Nacht

Neal Barrett, Jr. is a writer of stuff. He's written practically everything from science fiction to comics to mysteries to historical markers. Recent work includes an upcoming *Batman* project and the hilarious *Dead Dog Blues*.

A student of the famed Barron Storey, *Omaha Perez's* work has appeared in Millennium's *Asylum* and *Prey For Us Sinners* from Fantaco.

SAN ANTONIO, TEXAS. CHRISTMAS EVE, 1949

IT DIDN'T USED TO GET ALL THAT COLD HERE IN WINTER.

A LOT OF THINGS DIDN'T *USED* TO BE...

HEILIGE NACHT

Story: NEAL BARRETT, JR. Art: OMAHA PEREZ Letters: CARRIE SPIEGLE

SCHNEE, HERR GENERAL! ES IST SCHNEE!
NEIN, NEIN. DU HAST BIN GETRINKEN DER SCHNAPS, PAULI. IST NICHT DER SCHNEE MACHEN IN SAN ANTONIO!
WILST DU LOOKEN, HERR GENERAL? HIER--IST--DER--SCHNEE!
IST FOKKING SCHNEE!

YEEEEEEE-- HAW, HUNDER!

DANKE...DANKE SCHÖN, MEINE FREUNDE UND KAMARADEN... DAS IST EINE NACHT FÜR GELAUGHEN UND GUTE WILLEN...

...UND KRISTIMASS IS.. ESPECIALLEN FÜR DEM KINDER...

...FUR DEM LIEBLICH KINDER!

SINGEN, MEINE KINDER!

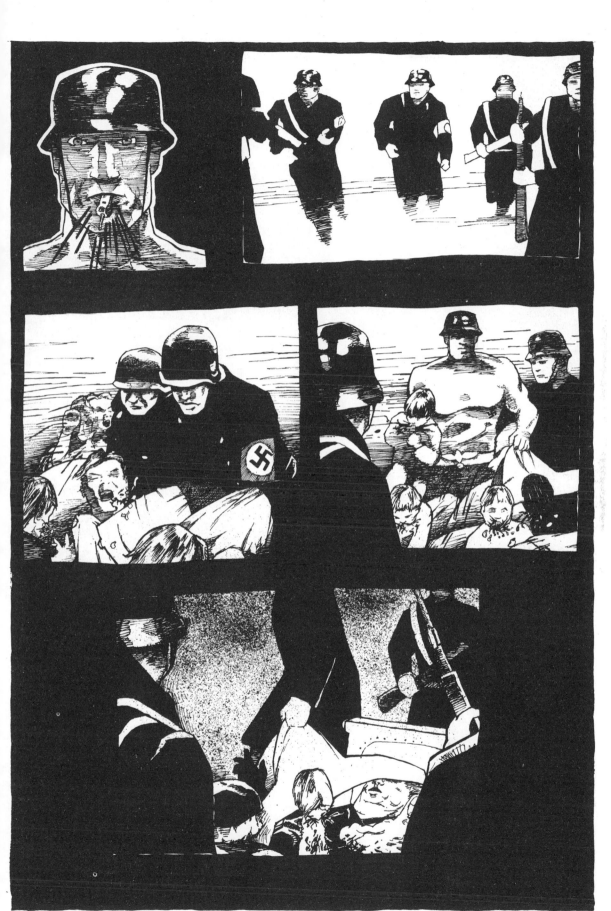

AHHHHHH...

Oil Of Dog

A war correspondent, fiction writer, and cynic, *Ambrose Bierce* was one of the great literary minds of the 19th century, who is as just as famous for his writing as for his death. His more famous works include *The Devil's Dictionary* and "The Occurrence at Owl Creek Bridge." *Occurrences*, an illustrated selection of Bierce's work, will appear in 1996 courtesy of Mojo Press.

The prolific *Neal Barrett, Jr.* has written nearly 1000 pages of comics. His comic book work includes adaptations of Andrew Vachss' stories for *Hard Looks* (Dark Horse) and of Joe R. Lansdale's stories for *By Bizarre Hands* (Dark Horse) and *The Wild West Show* (Mojo Press).

A frequent contributer to Fantagraphic's *Duplex Planet* and *The New Yorker*, *Dean Rohrer* is a professional artist living in New Jersey. He frequently illustrates books and covers for university presses.

OIL OF DOG

BY AMBROSE BIERCE

MY NAME IS BOFFER BINGS. I WAS BORN OF HONEST PARENTS IN ONE OF THE HUMBLER WALKS OF LIFE, MY FATHER BEING A MANUFACTURER OF DOG-OIL AND MY MOTHER HAVING A SMALL STUDIO IN THE SHADOW OF THE VILLAGE CHURCH, WHERE SHE DISPOSED OF UNWELCOME BABES...

ADAPTED BY NEAL BARRETT, JR.

ILLUSTRATION BY DEAN ROHRER

IN MY BOYHOOD I WAS TRAINED TO HABITS OF INDUSTRY; I NOT ONLY ASSISTED MY FATHER IN PROCURING DOGS FOR HIS VATS, BUT WAS FREQUENTLY EMPLOYED BY MY MOTHER TO CARRY AWAY THE DEBRIS OF HER WORK IN THE STUDIO.

IN PERFORMANCE OF THIS DUTY I SOMETIMES HAD NEED OF ALL MY NATURAL INTELLIGENCE, FOR ALL THE LAW OFFICERS IN THE VICINITY WERE OPPOSED TO MY MOTHER'S BUSINESS.

1

MY FATHER'S BUSINESS OF MAKING DOG-OIL WAS,
NATURALLY, LESS UNPOPULAR, THOUGH THE OWNERS
OF MISSING DOGS SOMETIMES REGARDED HIM WITH
SUSPICION...

...THIS UNREASONABLE ATTITUDE OF
THE TOWNSFOLK WAS REFLECTED, TO
SOME EXTENT, UPON ME.

MY FATHER HAD, AS SILENT PARTNERS, ALL THE
PHYSICIANS IN TOWN, WHO SELDOM WROTE A
PRESCRIPTION, OR ADMINISTERED A SOOTHING
ELIXER, WHICH DID NOT CONTAIN WHAT THEY
WERE PLEASED TO DESIGNATE AS OL. Can.

IT IS REALLY THE MOST VALUABLE MED-
ICINE EVER DISCOVERED, BUT MOST
PERSONS ARE UNWILLING TO MAKE
PERSONAL SACRIFICES FOR THE
AFFLICTED, AND IT WAS EVIDENT THAT
MANY OF THE FATTEST DOGS IN TOWN
HAD BEEN FORBIDDEN TO PLAY WITH ME...

...A FACT WHICH PAINED MY YOUNG
SENSIBILITIES, AND AT ONE TIME CAME
NEAR TO DRIVING ME TO BECOME A PIRATE.

ONE EVENING WHILE PASSING MY FATHER'S OIL FACTORY WITH THE BODY OF A FOUNDLING FROM MY MOTHER'S STUDIO, I SAW A CONSTABLE WHO SEEMED TO BE CLOSELY WATCHING MY MOVEMENTS ...

I AVOIDED HIM BY DODGING INTO THE OILERY BY A SIDE DOOR WHICH HAPPENED TO STAND AJAR ...

I LOCKED THE DOOR AT ONCE AND WAS ALONE WITH MY DEAD. MY FATHER HAD RETIRED FOR THE NIGHT. THE ONLY LIGHT IN THE PLACE CAME FROM THE FURNACE, WHICH GLOWED A DEEP, RICH CRIMSON UNDER ONE OF THE VATS, CASTING RUDDY REFLECTIONS ON THE WALLS.

WITHIN THE CAULDRON THE OIL STILL ROLLED IN INDOLENT EBULLITION, OCCASIONALLY PUSHING TO THE SURFACE A PIECE OF DOG.

THE NEXT DAY, MY FATHER INFORMED ME AND MY MOTHER THAT HE HAD OBTAINED THE FINEST QUALITY OF OIL THAT WAS EVER SEEN; THAT THE PHYSICIANS TO WHOM HE HAD SHOWN SAMPLES HAD SO PRONOUNCED IT. HE ADDED THAT HE HAD NO KNOWLEDGE AS TO HOW THE RESULTS HAD BEEN OBTAINED, THAT THE DOGS INVOLVED WERE OF AN ORDINARY BREED.

I DEEMED IT MY DUTY TO EXPLAIN, WHICH I DID, THOUGH PALSIED WOULD HAVE BEEN MY TONGUE IF I COULD HAVE FORSEEN THE CONSEQUENCES...

BEWAILING THEIR PREVIOUS IGNORANCE OF THE ADVANTAGES OF COMBINING THEIR INDUSTRIES, MY PARENTS AT ONCE TOOK MEASURES TO REPAIR THE ERROR. MY MOTHER REMOVED HER STUDIO TO A WING OF THE FACTORY BUILDING AND MY DUTIES IN CONNECTION WITH THE BUSINESS CEASED.

I WAS NO LONGER REQUIRED TO DISPOSE OF THE BODIES OF THE SMALL SUPERFLUOUS, AND THERE WAS NO NEED OF ALLURING DOGS TO THEIR DOOM, FOR MY FATHER DISCARDED THEM ALTOGETHER, THOUGH THEY STILL HAD AN HONORABLE PLACE IN THE NAME OF THE OIL...

5

SO SUDDENLY THROWN INTO IDLENESS, I MIGHT NATURALLY HAVE BEEN EXPECTED TO BECOME VICIOUS AND DISSOLUTE, BUT I DID NOT. THE HOLY INFLUENCE OF MY DEAR MOTHER WAS EVER ABOUT ME TO PROTECT ME FROM THE TEMPTATIONS WHICH BESET YOUTH, AND MY FATHER WAS A DEACON OF THE CHURCH.

ALAS, THAT THROUGH MY FAULT THESE ESTIMABLE PERSONS SHOULD HAVE COME TO SO BAD AN END!

FINDING A DOUBLE PROFIT IN HER BUSINESS, MY MOTHER NOW DEVOTED HERSELF TO IT WITH A NEW ASSIDUITY. SHE REMOVED NOT ONLY SUPERFLUOUS AND UNWELCOME BABES TO ORDER, BUT WENT OUT INTO THE HIGHWAYS AND BYWAYS, GATHERING IN CHILDREN OF A LARGER GROWTH, AND EVEN SUCH ADULTS AS SHE COULD ENTICE TO THE OILERY

MY FATHER, TOO, ENAMORED OF THE SUPERIOR QUALITY OF THE OIL PRODUCED, PURVEYED FOR HIS VATS WITH DILIGENCE AND ZEAL. THE CONVERSION OF THEIR NEIGHBORS INTO DOG-OIL BECAME, IN SHORT, THE ONE PASSION IN THEIR LIVES.

SO ENTERPRISING HAD THEY NOW BECOME THAT A PUBLIC MEETING WAS HELD, AND RESOLUTIONS PASSED SEVERELY CENSURING THEM. IT WAS INTIMATED THAT ANY FURTHER RAIDS UPON THE POPULATION WOULD BE MET IN A SPIRIT OF HOSTILITY...

MY POOR PARENTS LEFT THE MEETING BROKEN-HEARTED, DESPERATE AND, I BELIEVE, NOT ALTOGETHER SANE. ANYHOW, I DEEMED IT PRUDENT NOT TO ENTER THE OILERY WITH THEM THAT NIGHT, BUT SLEPT OUTSIDE IN THE STABLE.

AT ABOUT MIDNIGHT SOME MYSTERIOUS IMPULSE CAUSED ME TO RISE AND PEER THROUGH A WINDOW INTO THE FURNACE-ROOM, WHERE I KNEW MY FATHER NOW SLEPT. THE FIRES WERE BURNING BRIGHTLY, AS IF THE FOLLOWING DAY'S HARVEST WAS EXPECTED TO BE ABUNDANT.

MY FATHER WAS NOT IN BED: HE HAD RISEN IN HIS NIGHTCLOTHES AND WAS PREPARING A NOOSE IN A STRONG CORD. FROM THE LOOKS WHICH HE CAST AT THE DOOR OF MY MOTHER'S BEDROOM I KNEW WELL THE PURPOSE THAT HE HAD IN MIND. SPEECHLESS AND MOTIONLESS WITH TERROR, I COULD DO NOTHING IN PREVENTION OR WARNING.

7

FOR ONE INSTANT THEY LOOKED INTO EACH OTHER'S BLAZING EYES AND THEN SPRANG TOGETH WITH INDESCRIBABLE FURY.

SUDDENLY THE DOOR OF MY MOTHER'S APARTMENT WAS OPENED, NOISELESSLY, AND THE TWO CONFRONTED EACH OTHER, BOTH APPARENTLY SURPRISED. THE LADY, ALSO, WAS IN HER NIGHTCLOTHES, AND SHE HELD IN HER RIGHT HAND THE TOOL OF HER TRADE, A LONG, NARROW-BLADED DAGGER...

SHE, TOO, HAD BEEN UNABLE TO DENY HERSELF THE LAST PROFIT WHICH THE UNFRIENDLY ACTION OF THE CITIZENS HAD LEFT HER.

ROUND AND ROUND THE ROOM THEY STRUGGLED, THE MAN CURSING, THE WOMAN SHRIEKING, BOTH FIGHTING LIKE DEMONS – SHE TO STRIKE WITH THE DAGGER, HE TO STRANGLE HER WITH HIS GREAT BARE HANDS...

MY FATHER'S BREAST AND MY MOTHER'S WEAPON SHOWED EVIDENCE OF CONTACT FOR ANOTHER INSTANT THEY GLARED AT EACH OTHER IN THE MOST UNAMIABLE WAY.

I KNOW NOT HOW LONG I HAD THE UNHAPPINESS TO OBSERVE THIS DISAGREEABLE INSTANCE OF DOMESTIC INFELICITY, BUT AT LAST, AFTER A MORE THAN USUALLY VIGOROUS STRUGGLE, THE COMBATANTS SUDDENLY MOVED APART.

...THEN MY POOR, WOUNDED FATHER, UNMINDFUL OF RESISTANCE, REACHED OUT TO GRASP MY DEAR MOTHER IN HIS ARMS...

...COLLECTING ALL HIS FAILING ENERGIES, HE DRAGGED HER TO THE RIM OF THE BOILING CAULDRON, AND SPRANG IN WITH HER!

9

IN A MOMENT, BOTH HAD DISAPPEARED AND WERE ADDING THEIR OIL TO THAT OF THE COMMITTEE OF CITIZENS WHO HAD CALLED THE DAY BEFORE WITH AN INVITATION TO THE PUBLIC MEETING.

CONVINCED THAT THESE UNHAPPY EVENTS CLOSED TO ME EVERY AVENUE TO AN HONORABLE CAREER IN THAT TOWN, I REMOVED TO THE FAMOUS CITY OF OTUMWEE, WHERE THESE MEMOIRS ARE WRITTEN WITH A HEART FULL OF REMORSE FOR A HEEDLESS ACT ENTAILING SO DISMAL A COMMERCIAL DISASTER.

Photo by Beth Gwinn

In Memory Of
Robert Bloch